Interpretationshilfen

Richard III

William Shakespeare

Cornelsen

Richard III · Interpretationshilfen
Erarbeitet von Martina Baasner

Verlagsredaktion
Dr. Jan Dreßler

Umschlaggestaltung
Cornelsen Verlag Design / klein & halm Grafikdesign

Umschlagillustration
mauritius images/alamy stock photo/eye 35; Fotolia/Stefan Sottrell

Technische Umsetzung
L101 Mediengestaltung, Fürstenwalde

www.cornelsen.de

1. Auflage, 1. Druck 2019

Druck: AZ Druck und Datentechnik GmbH, Kempten

ISBN 978-3-06-035915-8

PEFC/04-31-2260

PEFC zertifiziert
Dieses Produkt stammt aus nachhaltig bewirtschafteten Wäldern und kontrollierten Quellen.

www.pefc.de

Contents

William Shakespeare 5
Historical Background 7
The Story 19
The Characters 42
Themes 56
Performance History and Criticism 59
Adaptations and Spin-offs 63
Language, Style and Dramatic Devices 65
Coping with Exam Papers 75
Written Test 83

All page and line numbers refer to the Cornelsen edition of Richard III (ISBN 978-3-06-036167-0) with the exception of cross-references to other sections of this book.

William Shakespeare (1564–1616)

Surprisingly little is known about William Shakespeare, Britain's national poet and Man of the Millennium, considering that he is probably the most famous playwright who ever lived. He was born in Stratford-upon-Avon in April 1564 and educated in the local grammar school. His father was a glove maker and a member of the town council. At 18, he married Anne Hathaway, with whom he had three children, Susanna, and the twins Hamnet and Judith. Little else is known about him until 1592, when Shakespeare is mentioned as being a playwright in London. It is also known that he worked as an actor and that he was part owner of a company of actors called 'The Lord Chamberlain's Men', who soon became the leading London theatre company and enjoyed Queen Elizabeth's patronage. After her death in 1603, King James also awarded them a royal patent and the troupe was renamed 'The King's Men'. Shakespeare became a wealthy man and bought properties in London and Stratford. He retired to Stratford in around 1614 and died there on 23 April 1616.

During his lifetime he wrote 38 plays. He may have written more but these have not survived. Although 18 of his plays were published during his lifetime, most of these editions (called 'Quartos') were probably not overseen by Shakespeare. Their texts may have been reconstructed from memory by members of the cast of the plays. It was only in 1623 that his plays were first published by two of his former colleagues in what is called 'The First Folio'. But as Shakespeare was by then dead, it cannot be said that the Folio is a definitive text. However, it was the first time that many of his plays, including *Richard III*, were printed. Shakespeare is unusual in that he wrote a wide variety of plays. Not only did he write history plays that covered over a hundred years of English history when the two Houses of Plantagenet fought for the crown, he was also equally competent at tragedy (e.g. *Hamlet*) as well as comedy (e.g. *Much Ado about Nothing*). Shakespeare was very good at turning older plays or stories from Greek or Roman mythology into new plays. Besides being a playwright, he was also a prolific poet: he wrote a cycle of 154 sonnets as well as several long poems.

Shakespeare's reputation grew slowly after his death, but by the end of the 20th century he had become the most performed dramatist in the world. Some theatre companies have been devoting their repertoire almost exclusively to the performance of his plays, such as Shakespeare's Globe in London or the Royal Shakespeare Company (RSC) in Stratford-upon-Avon. There are annual international festivals in his name and British institutions, such as the BBC and the British Council, produce media to help people understand his language and to facilitate an approach to his dramas. Many of the lines from his plays and poems are still well known today. After his death, his works have inspired adaptations and spin-offs in different art forms throughout the centuries and they are still considered very relevant today. Shakespeare's characters and their relationships and conflicts have remained timeless, since he never judges human behaviour and experience, but shows them in a touching way audiences or readers can still relate to. He has also coined an astonishing number of new words and managed to evoke gripping moods while giving his characters definitive voices at the same time. His complex or heightened language makes use of many rhetorical figures that make his lines so memorable. It is thought that he has contributed thousands of words to the English language. Shakespeare's inventiveness and creativity laid the groundwork that helped English to become the universal language that it is today.

Historical Background

Life in Renaissance England

The term "Renaissance" means "rebirth" and refers to the revival of interest in ancient Greek and Roman culture, whose influence on Western civilizations had dwindled during the Middle Ages (roughly between 500 and 1400). Beginning in Italy in the 14th century, Renaissance ideas spread all over Europe and challenged people's traditional beliefs through inventions and discoveries. Nicolaus Copernicus and Galileo Galilei introduced the idea that the earth revolves around the sun and not the other way around, like claimed in the Bible. Johannes Gutenberg's printing press (invented around 1439) furthered education and the spreading of ideas among the classes formerly restricted to information coming only from the ruling elite and the Church. English explorers, such as Francis Drake or Walter Raleigh, discovered or colonized new worlds through their seafaring missions, bringing back exotic goods and tales of their adventures.

All this opened England to continental and global developments and had an impact on her society and culture, especially on literary movements and playwrights. Shakespeare had a singular gift of using old dramatic or epic forms and combining them with the experiences he had been exposed to.

He would make use of the concepts governing people's lives as well, such as the *Chain of Being*, a hierarchical system of divine order that must not be upset. At its top in heaven was God, with the king, the Head of State, as his representative on earth, and the Pope as Head of the Church. Below them, arranged in descending order, were placed the nobility, the middle classes, the lower classes, animals, plants and minerals like stones. If this order was disturbed by an unusual event like the killing of the king, the broken chain was equivalent to overall chaos which had to be set right again. If a nation had to endure an evil king, this was seen as a temporary punishment for its past crimes, which would be lifted by a redeemer who "cleansed" the country. In *Richard III*, the order is restored by the Earl of Richmond, who invades England with his troops to overthrow King Richard, who had illegally seized the throne and thereby broken the chain (V, 7). Another notion of the Elizabethan worldview was that all living beings were made of the four elements: water, earth, fire and air, which had a counterpart in liquid substances in the human body, called *Humours*. A person's temperament depended on the mixture of these humours of blood, melancholy, phlegm and choler. If "blood" was predominant, one would be cheerful, and respectively melancholic, phlegmatic or choleric. An even balance of the humours meant a good-tempered person. In Richard's case, the element of fire takes over to reign his feelings of impatience and rage, which makes him an extremely 'ill-humoured' man.

In astronomy, the theory of the old geocentric model with the earth at the centre of the universe had been connected to the *Signs of the Zodiac*, which were believed to be governing people's natures. Similarly important was the belief that Fate, or Fortune, was the main controlling force in life. Its representation was the image of *The Wheel of Fortune*: A person in a high position on top of the wheel could expect to move to a lower place or fall off the wheel altogether. Alternatively, his prospects could improve with a ride from a lower to a higher place. At the same time, due to the influence of Renaissance ideas, more humanistic beliefs in man's ability to control his own destiny existed. Yet, superstition was widespread, and many people believed in omens and supernatural elements. In this play, Shakespeare makes much use of omens and dreams which were thought to reveal the future (cf. Language, Style and Dramatic Devices, pp. 71–72). Whereas other Shakespearean plays deal more extensively with witches and ghosts, there is only one such scene in *Richard III* when his victims' spirits wish him ill luck before the Battle of Bosworth, in which he then loses his life (V, 5).

Thus, the Elizabethans were in a state of change, and insecurity paired with excitement about developments was common. The different groups in society who had similar aims or religious beliefs tried to assert their interests at a time when political parties didn't yet exist and the monarch had a system of spies to counteract suspected treason. As theatres were a meeting-place for huge crowds, their supervision and control were vital to the authorities. Life expectancy was short, many children did not survive their teenage years nor mothers childbirth, because many illnesses could not be cured. In addition, the plague regularly killed large numbers of people. The English economy relied on agriculture, and the majority of the population were poor labourers and farmers while a rising and socially mobile middle class tried to achieve the wealth and status of the nobility despite the rigid concept of the *Chain of Being*. Manufacturing and overseas trade with imports and exports made the merchants prosperous. Shakespeare himself was a wealthy landowner when he retired to his birthplace.

Women were seen as dependent on a male family member or their husbands, and their only occupations were to raise a family and run the household. Despite Queen Elizabeth I's position as a monarch, the women's lot in her country did not improve. Even the wives of the nobility did not fare better once their husbands lost power or died, which is the fate of all women in *Richard III*. Queen Margaret, the Duchess of York (Richard's mother) and Queen Elizabeth (King Edward IV's wife) deplore the loss of their husbands and children and have no way to gain control over their lives. Richard's wife, Lady Anne, is used as a pawn in his game of power politics and dies before him.

Capital punishments of political enemies or murders of family members are a common occurrence in *Richard III*. Brutal public executions were watched as entertainment by Elizabethan crowds, and violence was an integral part of everyday life.

Points to remember:

- Renaissance ideas spread from Italy to England in the 16th century and widened people's horizons in many ways and areas.
- The reawakened interest in ancient Greek and Roman literary works and mythology had a great impact on playwrights.
- People believed in a hierarchical system of order where everyone had his place (*Chain of Being*) and chaos would reign if anyone disturbed this structure.
- Elizabethans believed in the concepts of the *Four Humours*, the *Signs of the Zodiac* and the *Wheel of Fortune*.
- All levels of society were spied upon by the monarch's secret agents.
- Life expectancy was short as there were only few cures for illnesses.
- Overseas trade and colonization brought wealth to the merchants, but the country's economy was based on agriculture and the farmers were poor.

- Women were not independent and had to obey men, they were seen as mothers and housewives only.
- Executions were frequent spectacles and crowds watched them for entertainment.

Queen Elizabeth

Queen Elizabeth I, the daughter of Tudor King Henry VIII and his second wife, Anne Boleyn, ruled England for 45 years from 1558 to 1603 in a time of relative prosperity and peace. Her father had broken ties with the Pope and the Catholic Church in order to divorce his first wife and founded the Anglican (Protestant) Church, of which he pronounced himself the Head. Elizabeth's half-sister Mary ruled before her and made Catholicism the state religion again. When Elizabeth became queen, she was regarded as an illegitimate child and consequently an illegitimate monarch by many Catholics. She continued her father's religious politics, and Anglicanism has since remained the official state religion. However, religious conflict determined English life throughout her reign, and she was declared a heretic by Rome in 1569, which endangered her claim to the throne. Her life was attempted more than once, and some of her aristocrats rebelled against her reign, although the divine right of kings to absolute rule was a doctrine Elizabethans strongly believed in. Elizabeth never married and avoided allying her throne with a foreign country or a domestic political group which might diminish her power. The defeat of the Spanish fleet (*Armada*) sent to overthrow her in 1588 led to England's supremacy on the seas.

Elizabeth travelled through her country, inviting herself into the houses of the aristocrats, many of whom she rewarded with important positions at court. The Crown had a reputation for the corruption of the courtiers who wanted to increase their influence. Members of the nobility were intent on living in luxury and acquiring as much land as possible. When *Richard III* was shown on stage in the early 1590s, Queen Elizabeth was more than 60 years old and her succession was unclear, since she had no heirs. By reminding his audience of the 'Wars of the Roses' and of the consequences of rival lords making claims to the throne after a monarch's death, Shakespeare might have intended to warn the aristocracy of the dangers of a similar situation.

In 1603, the crown passed to the queen's cousin James VI, King of Scotland, who converted from Catholicism to Anglicanism. His mother, Mary Stuart, Queen of Scots, had been executed for treason against the English throne. Her son became England's King James I and ruled from 1603 to 1625 (Shakespeare died in 1616). His reign was troubled by political and religious controversy, the most famous incident of which was the Gunpowder Plot in 1605, an attempt to assassinate the king.

Renaissance humanists thought that a leader had to be virtuous in order to guarantee a safe political environment. In contrast, the Italian statesman and philosopher Niccolò Machiavelli (1469–1527) claimed in his book *Il Principe* (*The Prince*, ~ 1513) that a ruler should be crafty and amoral in his politics if the end justified the means. In this regard, Richard can also be seen as an embodiment of this archetype, whose viciousness is meant to serve his own ambition only.

Points to remember:

- Queen Elizabeth I continued her father Henry VIII's religious politics and kept England Protestant.
- She faced opposition from the Pope and Catholics in her country and abroad in regard to the legitimacy of her rulership.
- Despite rebellions and attempts on her life the queen ruled for 45 years, and she never married.
- Her courtiers lived a life in luxury and corruption at court was commonplace.
- After Queen Elizabeth's death in 1603, the son of the Scottish queen Mary Stuart became England's new King James I.
- Richard is a Machiavel, a calculating politician working for his own ends.

The History Plays

The historical conflict between the Houses of Lancaster and York, who both belonged to the royal dynasty named 'Plantagenet', started in 1399 when the Lancastrian Henry Bolingbroke deposed the rightful King Richard II and seized the throne to become Henry IV. The conflict culminated in a series of civil wars called the 'Wars of the Roses' (1455–1487), as each family had a rose as their county's symbol: a white rose for Yorkshire and a red one for Lancashire.

From roughly 1589 to 1599, Shakespeare wrote a series of eight plays about these violent struggles, beginning with *Richard II*, two *Henry IV* plays, *Henry V*, three parts of *Henry VI* and finally *Richard III*, though he did not write them in this historically correct chronological order. The first series of four plays (= a tetralogy) was written early in the 1590s and consists of the three parts of *Henry VI* and *Richard III*. He finished the second tetralogy of *Richard II*, the two parts of *Henry IV* and *Henry V* in 1599. Aiming at a dramatization of historical events and telling a gripping story to engage his spectators, Shakespeare took great liberties with facts or the characters' portraits and compressed years of history into short spans of time in order to fit his purpose. Richard's two years of kingship are described as happening in less than a month, and the events leading up to his coronation shown on stage actually took place within 14 years.

To the playwright, it was more fascinating to present a detailed portrayal of the central character and to analyse his motivation than to give a historically accurate account of events. In their arguments, Shakespeare has the characters of *Richard III* refer to historical events known to his audience and shown in the preceding plays and blame each other for their past crimes and acts of cruelty. Both the Lancastrians and Yorkists are guilty of destructive violence and family betrayals, which have a vital effect on the play's present, as they now pay the price for their sins.

By winning the Battle of Bosworth (1485) and killing King Richard III, Henry Tudor, the Earl of Richmond (Lancaster), ended the decades of civil strife between the Houses of Lancaster and York and established the Tudor dynasty. He married the former King Edward IV's daughter, Elizabeth York, and thereby reconciled the two warring families. The two different coloured roses then appeared united in the new dynasty's coat of arms. Since his personal claim to the throne – as a distant cousin of King Henry VI – was not seen as overly strong, Richmond, then King Henry VII, encouraged biographers to show him as a heroic liberator. Thus, to support the Tudors, Elizabethan writers of historical chronicles have defamed Richard III as an evil king whose deposition was justified, which historians have called the 'Tudor Myth'. Thomas More's book *The History of King Richard the Thirde* (1557) also portrays Richard in this negative vein, and Shakespeare based his protagonist's portrait on this interpretation. Back then, history books were not as reliable as they are today. As Queen Elizabeth I's grandfather Henry VII (Richmond) ended Richard III's rule and the play was written during her reign, it is possible that Shakespeare followed More's example to gain favour.

To great acclaim, the BBC adapted Shakespeare's history plays in a TV series called *The Hollow Crown* (2012–2016), starring several well-known actors, such as Ben Whishaw, Jeremy Irons, Tom Hiddleston or Judi Dench. The role of Richard III was played by Benedict Cumberbatch.

Points to remember:

- Shakespeare wrote eight plays about the historical struggle for the throne between two hostile branches of the royal Plantagenet dynasty, the Houses of York and Lancaster, that culminated in the 'Wars of the Roses' (1455–1485).
- *Richard III* is the final play of this series and depicts the Yorkist King Richard's ascension to the throne and his subsequent downfall brought about by Richmond, a Lancastrian, who then united the two warring Houses and founded the Tudor dynasty.
- Shakespeare ignored historical reality and adjusted the events and portraits of personalities to his needs as a dramatist, e.g. by shortening the actual time spans of reigns.
- Henry VII (Richmond) had only a shaky claim to the throne and encouraged biographers to blacken Richard III's name in historical chronicles in order to strengthen his own position and justify his actions. This biased view of history is called the 'Tudor Myth'.
- Having only unreliable sources and maybe in an attempt to please Queen Elizabeth I, who was Richmond's descendant, Shakespeare reflected this negative image of Richard.

The theatre

The first commercial theatre in England, simply called 'The Theatre', was built in 1576 by James Burbage, who would later become Shakespeare's associate. The London Common Council forbade theatres within the city walls, and people commonly regarded actors and playwrights as low-life characters, little better than criminals. Next to the theatre buildings outside the city other entertainments, such as taverns, brothels, cockfighting or bear-baiting arenas, were situated. Burbage built his theatre on the shore of the Thames River, in Shoreditch. However, Shakespeare and his actors managed to secure the patronage of a nobleman and later even that of the monarch. They became popular entertainment at Queen Elizabeth's and King James' court. Their financial success gave Shakespeare and his shareholders the funds to build the Globe playhouse in 1599. There, James Burbage's son Richard, Will Kempe, Edward Alleyn and other players performed in the plays Shakespeare wrote for them during many years and established their excellent reputation.

Shakespeare may have found his love for the theatre by watching travelling acting companies who came to the countryside where he lived before he moved to London. The troupes would transport their property on wagons and use inns or courtyards to perform their plays, because no buildings for theatres existed. They mostly showed religious stories or scenes taken from the Bible which meant to teach viewers a lesson in morals. Richard can be seen as a stereotypical character embodying evil in humankind ('Vice') and serve as an example of how not to behave as a proper Christian. He even refers to this stage representation ironically: '*Thus, like the formal Vice, Iniquity, I moralize* (= interpret) *two meanings in one word.*' (III, i, ll. 83–84) During the Renaissance, the plays would become less religious and would be based on Greek or Roman legends or have historical events as their plot.

The Master of the Revels, a public official, had to read and approve every play to be performed and could shut down a theatre completely. During times of plague or social or political riots, authorities would close the theatres, which they feared were places of moral corruption. Audiences were packed with people from all walks of life – it is said that a full house at the Globe numbered about 3,000 spectators. The rich patrons sat on the stage or on gallery seats, whereas the poorer visitors called 'groundlings' stood in front of the stage that was about a metre above the ground. These 'groundlings' paid a penny for the entertainment, which was a day's wage. Audience behaviour was quite different then, with people eating, drinking and smoking during the performance and heckling players or even throwing things at them. Shakespeare wrote for his diverse audience and adjusted his language and the characters, actions and situations so as to appeal to all levels of his society.

The theatre buildings were round and roofless with a thrust stage (projecting out into the audience), and plays were staged during the day. A performance could take half a day – today Shakespeare's plays are usually cut because they can last up to four hours. The sets were bare and props would be carried on by the players in full view of the audience, because there were no breaks or intervals. If a scene was set at night, the actors would comment on the moon or stars in the sky to indicate the hour of the day. The actors did not wear the costumes indicated for the time the plays were set in, but their normal clothes. However, they had elegant hand-me-down clothes from the upper classes for royalty shown on stage.

Most plays were rehearsed for just a day or two, they ran only for a short time and players had to learn their parts for a new play quickly. Full scripts did not exist, but the actors only had their own lines on paper slips with the cues of the previous speaker so that they knew when to say their lines. Some theatres staged up to four different plays within a week. Female roles were performed by boys and young men, because women were not permitted to act on stage until 1660. As Shakespeare often used the motif of cross-dressing, when female characters (played by boys) dressed as boys on stage, this allowed much room for double meaning.

The Globe burned down in 1613 after the roof caught fire when a cannon was fired during a performance. In the 1990s, a reconstruction of the old Globe was built very close to its original site, where visitors today can experience plays the way Elizabethans did.

In 1642, the Puritans, a very strict religious faction that saw performing and watching plays as immoral, succeeded in closing the theatres altogether. They did not reopen until Charles II came to the throne 18 years later. By then, many of the theatrical traditions of Shakespeare's theatre were lost, and the new theatres of the Restoration period viewed and staged his plays very differently.

Points to remember:

- Theatres were not allowed within the London city walls because actors were thought of as vagabonds.
- Shakespeare must have seen travelling players in Stratford who performed simple stories, e.g. from the Bible.
- In London, his troupe secured royal patronage.
- Their company built the Globe playhouse in 1599, which burnt down in 1613.
- Shakespeare wrote his plays for a very diverse audience and adjusted language and action to appeal to everyone.
- During riots or outbreaks of the plague, the theatres would be closed since they held so many people.
- A censor, called the Master of the Revels, had to approve each play for the performance on stage.
- Performances took place during the day, and time and place of the scenes were indicated by the dialogue; scene changes did not exist.
- Actors only had their parts on a slip of paper, there were no full scripts.
- Rehearsal time was just a few days, and some theatres put on up to four plays a week.
- Women were not allowed on stage, and their roles were played by boys and young men.
- In 1642, the Puritans, a strict religious sect, were successful in shutting down all theatres which reopened only in 1660.
- Close to the original site, a reconstruction of the old Globe was built in the 1990s.

English Renaissance drama

In medieval times, plays took the form of folk tales or stories from the Christian tradition which were meant to strengthen people's belief in religion and to teach them moral behaviour. In the 'Mystery Plays', dramatic Bible scenes were re-enacted. 'Morality Plays' with their stock situation of the fight between good and evil (or 'Virtue' and 'Vice'), in which the good character invariably wins after having been severely tempted by the devilish character, were very popular for hundreds of years. The other characters were allegories or personifications of positive and negative human qualities, such as Strength, Charity, Mercy or Greed, Lust and Envy, which were shown in a dilemma the viewers could relate to. Gradually, plays would feature more secular content and show characters with more personal struggles in the so-called 'Interludes' of the 16th century. The reawakened interest in Greek and Roman literary forms had its influence too, and comedies, tragedies and other literary texts by classical authors such as Plautus, Seneca, Plutarch and Ovid were inspiration and models for dramatists. *Richard III* is modelled on Greek tragedy inasmuch as typical features, such as a Chorus of wailing women who comment on the action and bemoan the sorrow put on them, are introduced. Violence and bloodshed usually happened offstage and were only reported or could be inferred from the characters' words. Here, only Clarence's knife injury and Richard's death in combat are performed on stage. Equally following classical dramatic plots, the criminal hero step by step overcomes all obstacles until he triumphs before his eventual downfall.

Shakespeare's plots owe debt as well to other Renaissance playwrights preceding his career, such as Thomas Kyd (1558–1594) or Christopher Marlowe (1564–1593), who had written very popular plays. Kyd's *Spanish Tragedy*, a very bloody tale of vengeance, contained elements such as extremes of emotion, deception, revenge and justice, which can also be found in *Richard III*. Marlowe's dramatic works *Tamburlaine the Great*, *The Jew of Malta* and *Dr Faustus* threw a spotlight on strong characters who had complex personalities and experienced conflicting emotions, like all of Shakespeare's tragic heroes.

Points to remember:

- In the Middle Ages, 'Mystery Plays' (Biblical scenes) and 'Morality Plays' (allegorical characters struggling with temptation) were popular for a long time.
- More secular plays called 'Interludes' showing individual characters replaced the religious plays in the 16th century.

- Elizabethan playwrights looked to classical Greek and Roman plays and literary texts for inspiration.
- *Richard III* contains typical elements of Greek tragedy, such as the use of chorus-like characters, little violence shown on stage and the protagonist's slow but steady path to personal victory followed by his destruction.
- Thomas Kyd and Christopher Marlowe were successful dramatists and made characters display extreme emotions on stage.

Shakespeare's sources

Shakespeare's main source for the play was Raphael Holinshed's *The Chronicles of England, Scotlande, and Irelande*, a history book that was published in two volumes in 1577 (2nd ed. 1587). Other sources focussing on the warring families were Edward Hall's *The Union of the Two Noble and Illustre Famelies of Lancastre and Yorke* (1548) as well as the *Mirour for Magistrates* (1574), edited by William Baldwin and George Ferrers. Sir Thomas More's book *The History of King Richard the Thirde* (1557), in which Richard is described as a witty villain with much irony, was another inspiration (cf. p. 13).

The Story

Richard III is the story of a medieval despot who upsets the divine right of kings by killing off all the lineal heirs to the English throne before him so that he can seize it. Since Richard cannot fit into society, he turns into a force of pure evil, taking cruel revenge on everybody with whom he has a bone to pick. With witty monologues and his diabolical charisma, he can equally fascinate and repulse the audience by his machinations. Once he has supreme power, however, the crown changes him and he loses his grip. His demands on his followers as well as a rising opposition lead to his well-merited fall and the establishment of a new reigning dynasty. Apart from telling Richard's story, the play is also about political intrigues and how far people are ready to go when committing horrible crimes if they don't have to fear any retribution.

In the series of history plays, in which Shakespeare dramatizes the violent struggle between the two noble families of York and Lancaster (the 'Wars of the Roses'), *Richard III* is the final play. Though belonging to the same royal dynasty of the Plantagenets, the members of the two branches of the family fought bitterly to seize the throne from 1398 to 1485. The action of the play runs from 1471 to 1485, when the Lancastrian Henry, Earl of Richmond, defeats King Richard III in the Battle of Bosworth and, by marrying the last Yorkist princess, unites the Houses of York and Lancaster and rules as the first Tudor monarch Henry VII.

Act I

Scene 1: The Yorkists have just beaten the Lancastrians in the Battle of Tewkesbury when the play begins. The oldest of the three victorious brothers, Edward, has become the new King of England. The middle brother, George, Duke of Clarence (as he is called throughout the play), has earlier turned against his family and joined the Lancastrians' cause because he is critical of King Edward IV's wife, Elizabeth Woodville. At this point, he is reconciled with the king, but George's reputation as a turncoat lingers. The youngest brother, Richard, Duke of Gloucester, supported Edward's claim to the throne during the wars, but now he feels alienated from everyone around him celebrating peacetime. The first scene is set in a London street, where Richard enters alone and discloses his true feelings in a monologue. First, he compares the past war to the present peaceful times. He hates idleness and does not enjoy courting ladies because he thinks himself ugly due to his deformity, which he describes in brutally honest terms (cf. Characters, pp. 43–44). Instead, by plotting against others, he wants to '*prove a villain*' (l. 30) to pass the time and amuse himself. Turning the listeners or readers into his accomplices, Richard informs them of his plan to sow mistrust and hatred between King Edward and their brother George. He has already spread rumours about a prophecy that Edward's heirs will be killed by a murderer whose name begins with 'G', which allegedly signifies George. Ironically, Richard's ducal name of Gloucester also begins with a 'G', and it will be him who later orders the death of Edward's sons. In his speech, which serves as an exposition, Richard sets the scene (time, place, and atmosphere), conveys his state of mind and attitude towards others and discloses his plans to deceive them ('*plots have I laid*', l. 32).

At this moment, on his way to the king's prison, the Tower, Clarence enters guarded by Sir Robert Brakenbury and an escort. He is to be imprisoned by order of Edward IV who fears the false prophecy invented by Richard might come true. With fake sympathy, Richard suggests that Queen Elizabeth (Elizabeth Woodville, widow of Sir John Grey) and her brother, Earl Rivers (Anthony Woodville) are responsible for his imprisonment, since they have already persuaded the king to send his Lord Chamberlain, Lord Hastings, to the Tower. Richard also insinuates that the king's mistress, Jane Shore, equally has an influence on King Edward against which he and Clarence must guard themselves. Queen Elizabeth was a commoner and the king gave titles to her relatives, which rankled the old aristocratic families. Brakenbury, the Lieutenant of the Tower, interrupts the conversation to say that Clarence must not speak to anyone, whereupon Richard pretends that their talk was harmless. He promises his brother to do everything possible to obtain his release from jail, which Clarence takes at face value. But Richard shows his duplicity when he says, '*I will deliver you or lie for you*' (l. 115). He mentioned his plot to incriminate Clarence at the beginning of the scene, and his words are a cruel pun on the fate he devises for his brother: *I will deliver you* (= set you free / hand you over to the king) *or lie for you* (= take your place in prison / lie in wait for you (i.e., in order to attack you)). As soon as Clarence has left, Richard congratulates himself gleefully and says that he will see to it that '*simple, plain Clarence*' dies (ll. 118–119), thereby proving that he is cold-blooded and unscrupulous enough to have his own brother killed.

Recently freed from the Tower, Hastings appears next and informs Richard of King Edward's declining health and the doctors' fear for his life. Richard feigns being worried and blames the king's poor health on the latter's excessive lifestyle. After the Lord Chamberlain has left for the palace, Richard reveals his intention to blacken Clarence's name even further so that the king will soon order Clarence's execution before dying himself. A further wicked plan is to marry Lady Anne (Warwick's daughter), whose husband Edward, Prince of Wales, and father-in-law, King Henry VI, Richard has killed in the Battle of Tewkesbury. This is not done for the love for her, but for a secret purpose.

Analyse the means with which Shakespeare characterizes his protagonist.
What is the effect of Richard's sharing his plans with the audience?
Sum up the picture Richard paints of his two brothers' characters and the influence women have at court.

Scene 2: As the only mourner, Lady Anne follows the coffin of the late King Henry VI. She asks the bearers to set it down for a moment for her to grieve for him and lament his untimely death and that of his son, her husband Edward, Prince of Wales. Cursing Richard for killing both men, Anne wishes death on any children of his and his future wife to be as miserable as she is at present. Unwittingly, she thereby curses herself, as she will marry him despite her furious tirade against him. Richard enters and orders the funeral procession to halt again, as it has resumed its course meanwhile. This greatly angers Lady Anne, who berates him lengthily as a '*dreadful minister of hell*' (l. 46) and '*foul devil*' (l. 50), who has '*made the happy earth thy hell*' (l. 51). She is shocked to see King Henry's corpse beginning to bleed because ''*tis thy presence that exhales* (= causes to flow) *this blood*' (l. 58). Elizabethans believed that dead bodies would ooze blood in the presence of their murderers. Richard gently defends himself, denying at first that he was responsible for the Lancastrians' deaths and blaming his brother Edward for it. Then he claims that Anne's beauty was his motive for killing her husband so that he could marry her. When Anne spits at him in disgust, he offers her his sword to stab him in retaliation for his deed, but she cannot bring herself to do it, nor can she, at his request, repeat her demand that he should commit suicide to repent of his actions. Richard has surely calculated this seemingly dangerous risk and correctly figured that she would lack the nerve to use the sword against him. This grandiose gesture of a passionate suitor and spurned lover makes Anne hesitate in her attitude towards him. She relents, accepts the ring he offers her and leaves after he has promised her to take charge of the funeral personally. As soon as Richard is alone on stage, having directed the procession to a different place than originally intended, he gloats over his triumph: '*Was ever woman in this humour wooed? Was ever woman in this humour won? I'll have her, but I will not keep her long.*' (I, ii, ll. 224–226) In his merry mood, he plans to have new clothes made and reflects that he must be more attractive than he thought, which contrasts with his unfavourable self-description in I, 1. Richard is elated because, even under the most difficult circumstances, his sexual conquest and his performance as a con artist were successful. Anne becomes the Duchess of Gloucester, but regrets her decision later, especially when Richard is crowned king. He gets rid of her as soon as he is convinced that another woman is politically more advantageous to him than Anne.

This is a shocking and suspenseful scene to watch on stage, one of the emotional highlights of the play. Since Anne's complete change of opinion puzzles the spectators, there has been much speculation about her motives. The scene can be interpreted and played very differently: Anne could be seen as a naïve woman who is deceived by an obvious villain or, after having lost her male protectors, as a defenceless widow in need of a more secure societal position. Moreover, she could have been unable to resist Richard's 'bad boy' charm. All three options are not particularly becoming to Anne, who not only abandons the dead king she mourned so deeply but also remains unsure of how sincere Richard is: '*I would* (= wish) *I knew thy heart.*' (l. 193)

Explain why Anne, who can articulate her feelings so well, cannot match up with Richard and his skilful use of language and arguments.
What traits of character can you infer from what both Anne and Richard do and say?

Scene 3: In the royal palace, Queen Elizabeth worries greatly about her husband's health while her brother, Earl Rivers, and her son from a previous marriage, Earl Grey, try to reassure her. With Clarence in prison, in the event of King Edward's death, Richard, as the closest male relative of the young Prince of Wales (who will be Edward V), would rule as Lord Protector in his name. The Duke of Buckingham arrives to report that the king feels better and wants Richard and the Woodville faction, namely Elizabeth and her relatives, to reconcile. These hopes are dashed when Richard, upon his entry, immediately attacks the company present and accuses them of slandering him when talking to the king, proving Elizabeth's claim that he '*loves not me, nor none of you*' (l. 13). Richard quarrels with Elizabeth, blaming her for Clarence's and Hastings' imprisonment, and spitefully comments on '*great promotions [that] are daily given to ennoble those that scarce some two days since were worth a noble*' (ll. 79–81). Outraged by these insults, Elizabeth tells Richard she will inform the king of his scornful reproaches, which he dares her to do. Richard reminds her of his own support of Edward during the wars when '*to royalize his blood, I spent mine own*' (l. 123), whereas the Woodvilles supposedly betrayed the Yorkist cause. When Rivers points out that '*We followed then our lord, our sovereign king. So should we you, if you should be our king*' (ll. 145–146), Richard firmly rejects the idea that he should become king, hiding his true aims: '*I had rather be a pedlar. Far be it from my heart, the thought thereof!*' (ll. 147–148)

Unseen by the others, old Queen Margaret from the House of Lancaster enters, who is the widow of King Henry VI and the mother of the dead Prince of Wales, Edward of Westminster. She listens to the family quarrel and quietly rails against both Elizabeth and Richard in asides only to be heard by the audience. Margaret has been banished from England on pain of death but has come back to demand her return to the throne. When she speaks up, Richard reminds her of her own cruel deeds for which she now suffers God's punishment, and all others join in to condemn her, too. After having voiced her ancient grudges, Margaret condemns everyone individually, prophesying regret, sorrow, pain, loneliness, treason and early deaths. She curses Richard powerfully, but he turns the damnation against her by inserting Margaret's name instead of his own at the very end of her angry speech (ll. 214–238). The only one excepted from these ill wishes is Buckingham, whom Margaret warns of Richard, but when Buckingham scorns her, she foretells his downfall. The old queen's prophecies will come true, but this will be realized only when it is too late. Pretending to repent his part in Margaret's fate after she has left, Richard also acts the part of the religious man who blasphemously asks for God's pardon for those responsible for Clarence's arrest, which he himself plotted. Sir William Catesby summons the queen and courtiers to the king. Alone, Richard congratulates himself on his consummate performance of shifting the blame for Clarence's imprisonment on to the queen and the Woodvilles as well as sowing discord between them and his followers Buckingham, Hastings and Derby (Lord Stanley) or, as he calls them, '*many simple gulls*' (l. 326). He has also smartened up his public persona by showing Christian forgiveness to an enemy and quoting the Bible. Two murderers hired by him enter to fetch the warrant from Richard allowing them access to Clarence's cell. He tells them not to listen to the well-spoken Clarence imploring them not to kill him. The first murderer assures him they will not: '*Talkers are no good doers*' (l. 349), but do their business promptly.

Explain why the quarrel between the Woodvilles and Richard is taking up so much space in this scene.
Some directors have cut Margaret's part from their performance of the play. Assess what would be missing if her character did not appear.

Scene 4: In his prison cell, Clarence tells his jailer about the nightmare he has just awoken from. In his dream, he escaped from the Tower, sailed to Burgundy in France together with Richard and was accidentally knocked off the ship by his brother. In the water, he saw gold and jewels next to corpses on the seabed. He felt the pain of drowning and that of a soul in agony led to hell on its underwater journey. Accused by two men he betrayed and killed in the 'Wars of the Roses'

(Warwick and Edward, Prince of Wales) who sent howling furies to torment him, Clarence awoke and now regretfully confesses his misdeeds to the jailer. Clarence complains that he committed his sins for King Edward, who requites this now so unjustly, and he prays to God, asking him to punish only himself and to spare his family. The dream reveals that Clarence's subconscious mind is more aware of the mortal danger Richard poses to him than he admits to himself. The jailer, who has listened to him with sympathy, stays at his side when he falls back asleep. Next, the Lieutenant of the Tower, Brakenbury, enters, followed by the two murderers who take over the guard as indicated in their warrant. Brakenbury leaves to inform the king about this. When the murderers discuss whether Clarence should be killed while sleeping, the second murderer fears he will have to burn in hell for this. When Clarence awakes and guesses their intention correctly, he appeals to the murderers' conscience, pointing out that he has not yet been convicted of any crime and saying that God's judgement overrides that of a king. The assassins accuse Clarence of treason and murder committed during the wars, which he counters by saying that Edward was equally involved in killing the former royals. After Clarence has told the men that Richard will reward them for sparing his life, he cannot believe their reply that it is actually Richard who seeks his death. In a last effort to stop them, Clarence begs one of them for mercy directly: '*My friend, I spy some pity in thy looks*' (l. 255), but to no avail. The first murderer stabs him and puts his body offstage into a butt of Malmsey wine. Repenting his action, the second murderer tells the first one that he wants no payment from Richard.

Beside Richard's courtship of Lady Anne, this is the second highly charged scene in the first act which creates tension and has a deep impact on the viewers' emotions. Clarence's tormented soul, his loss of hope and fear of death evoke pity. Here, the serious consequences of Richard's villainy are drastically shown, while later cruelties in the play will take place offstage. Clarence's dream predicting his death (cf. Language, Style and Dramatic Devices, p. 72) is a vivid and poetic description of how Elizabethans imagined hell. His pitiful pleas for his life that go unheard and his wrestling with his own guilt make Clarence more likeable than many other characters in the play.

Analyse the effect Shakespeare wanted to achieve by describing the treasures and the dead bodies at the bottom of the sea in Clarence's dream.
Examine how the theme of 'Conscience' is treated in this scene.

Act II

Scene 1: King Edward, who expects to die soon, has assembled the hostile factions of his family in the palace and makes the Woodvilles swear loyalty to Hastings and Buckingham, who vow this in return. Richard enters and joins the reconciliation by promising friendly peace, claiming to have no enemies in England at all. When Queen Elizabeth asks the king to forgive Clarence as well, Richard shocks everyone with the news of Clarence's death. King Edward says he reversed the death sentence, but Richard explains that he was executed by the first order. Lord Stanley (earlier referred to as Derby) enters to beg the king the favour to pardon one of his men who killed another nobleman's servant. Edward grants this and laments that no one present pleaded for Clarence's life or spoke up for him. Extremely upset, he remembers his brother's good deeds and fears God's punishment for his lack of mercy. Richard uses the opportunity to remark how pale the queen and her '*guilty kindred*' (= relatives) looked and blames them for Clarence's demise (l. 138). King Edward's only appearance in the play fulfils the function to show what a good ruler deserving of the crown should be like.

Contrast Clarence's and Edward's character traits with those of their brother Richard.

Scene 2: This scene is often cut in performances because it does not move the action forward but focuses on the characters' reactions to events and their plans for the near future. In another room of the palace, Clarence's children (Margaret and Edward Plantagenet) worry about their father and ask their grandmother, the Duchess of York, if he is well. Citing Richard, the children blame the king for Clarence's arrest, but the Duchess warns them not to be deceived by their uncle and then admits that their father is dead. Queen Elizabeth enters with

Rivers and the Marquess of Dorset (her son by her previous husband) to report that King Edward has died. As Elizabeth did not mourn Clarence, the Duchess and her grandchildren feel little sympathy for Elizabeth's grief. The Duchess and the children express their own sorrow in highly patterned, ritualistic language (ll. 72–88) common in Greek tragedy (cf. Historical Background, p. 17). Realizing the need to quickly crown Elizabeth's eldest son in order to keep the Woodvilles in power, Rivers urges his sister not to lose time with grieving. When Richard enters with Buckingham and other courtiers to offer his condolences to Edward's wife and mother, he also asks the latter for her blessing. Buckingham suggests that Edward Prince of Wales (now Edward V) should be taken from their home in Ludlow to London for his coronation and be guarded by a small escort so as not to provoke civil unrest, which is approved by all. Alone, Richard and Buckingham decide to accompany the prince on his journey in order to separate him from the Woodvilles.

Compare the behaviour of Richard and the courtiers in this scene to what they promised and did in the previous scene.

Scene 3: On a London street, three citizens discuss the news of King Edward's death and share their worries about the country's future. They are not optimistic about a young ruler, though in the case of a former king all went well because he had wise and virtuous advisers. Now, however, the rivalry between the Woodvilles and Richard can only mean harm to their '*sickly land*' (l. 30).

Imagine you are an assistant director arguing for the omission of this scene in performance. Which points would you put forward in your evaluation?

Scene 4: In yet another room of the palace, Queen Elizabeth, her youngest son, the Duke of York (also named Richard), and the Duchess of York listen to the Archbishop of York's account of the Prince of Wales's journey to London, waiting for his imminent arrival. They talk about the boys of the Yorkist family growing up and the young duke refers to Richard's having been born with teeth. The quiet moment is contrasted with the shock caused by a messenger's bad news that Richard and Buckingham have sent Rivers, Grey and their follower Sir Thomas Vaughan to Pomfret Castle, a place used for executions. It is unknown why they have been imprisoned, but Elizabeth foresees the '*ruin of my house*' (l. 50) at Richard's hands. With her son, she seeks sanctuary in a church where she cannot be arrested. The Archbishop offers to give her protection and will conduct them there.

Point out how Richard has systematically disempowered the Woodville family. Examine the role of women and children in this act.

Act III

Scene 1: Richard, Buckingham and the Lord Mayor welcome Prince Edward and Cardinal Bourchier (the Archbishop of Canterbury who traditionally crowns the king) to London. Edward is troubled by the fact that his Woodville uncles have been arrested and that his mother and brother are not there to greet him. Hastings arrives to report that the queen has sought sanctuary. When Buckingham asks the Cardinal to persuade the queen to let her youngest son join his brother Edward, he refuses, citing '*the holy privilege of blessed sanctuary*' (ll. 42–43). Arguing that this does not apply to children who did not demand shelter themselves, Buckingham tells Hastings to bring the young Duke of York by force. Reluctantly, the Cardinal consents and both men depart. Hiding his real intentions, Richard recommends the princes to stay in the Tower (both a royal castle and a prison) for their own safety until the coronation will take place, which the prince is not enthusiastic about. When the men return with Edward's brother, the conversation becomes more light-hearted and the young duke jokes a little with Richard, whose replies are full of double meanings. For example, when the duke asks for his weapon, Richard says '*My dagger, little cousin? With all my heart*' (l. 112). The duke fears that Clarence's ghost haunts the Tower, but the prince says '*I fear no uncles dead*' (l. 147). Still, both leave with a heavy heart and only Richard, Buckingham and Catesby remain on stage to discuss their scheme of making Richard King of England. Catesby, who thinks Hastings will support Prince Edward as the future king, is sent to find out whether this is true and report back at once. Planning to hold two separate councils, one for Edward's coronation and the other for his own institution as king, Richard intends to undercut Edward's supporters even further. To lure Hastings over to the 'right side', Richard suggests to Buckingham to mention the upcoming executions of Rivers and Grey, who were Hastings' enemies. In case he does not join their conspiracy, Richard will '*chop off his head*' (l. 193). To reward Buckingham's loyalty, Richard promises him the Earldom of Hereford and Clarence's personal property.

Point out the strategies of power politics Richard makes use of in this scene.

Scene 2: At four o'clock in the morning, a messenger from Stanley knocks at Hastings' door to tell him of a dream his master had: '*He dreamt the boar* (Richard's emblem) *had razèd off his helm* (= helmet)' (l. 8), which he interprets as an attempt on his life. Stanley wants to flee to the north with Hastings because he dreads the results of the two councils. Mocking such worries, Hastings sends word back that no trouble is to be expected and Richard is no threat. Catesby arrives to sound Hastings out on a possible support of Richard's bid for the crown and learns that he will be loyal to King Edward's heir '*to the death*' (l. 52). However, Hastings is glad to hear that his opponents from the Woodville faction will be put to death, and believes he has Richard's support. When Stanley enters, still nervous and mistrustful about the two councils and the executions at Pomfret, he agrees to go to the Tower with Hastings. While leaving, Hastings encounters a Pursuivant (an official state manager) whom he last met on his way to prison. He gives him money for a drink and brags he is now '*in better state than e'er I was*' (l. 100). A priest enters whom Hastings promises payment for a religious service on the following Sunday. At this moment, Buckingham appears and tells Hastings he has no need for a priest, unlike the Pomfret prisoners. In an aside, he reminds the audience that Hastings will not survive the day. Together they go off to the Tower for dinner.

Outline the mistakes Hastings makes that seal his fate.
Analyse the use of effective dramatic irony in this scene.

Scene 3: At Pomfret Castle, Richard's follower Ratcliffe walks Rivers, Grey and Vaughan to their execution. Rivers tells Ratcliffe that they are innocent and recalls that another king, Richard II, was killed there, too. The deposition of the king from the throne in 1399 was the beginning of the long-lasting power struggle between the Houses of Lancaster and York (cf. Historical Background, pp. 11–13). The three prisoners remember Queen Margaret's curses and hope that the sinister prophecies for Richard, Hastings and Buckingham will be fulfilled as well and that no other Woodvilles may suffer.

This is the second short scene after II, 3 in which Shakespeare shows minor characters commenting on current or historical political situations. Explain the functions of this scene in the play.

Scene 4: In the Tower, a council consisting of the Bishop of Ely, Buckingham, Hastings, Stanley and other courtiers plans Prince Edward's coronation, but are waiting for Richard's approval. When he enters, Richard asks the Bishop to send for some strawberries, takes Buckingham aside to confirm Hastings' opposition to Richard's scheme and withdraws with him to discuss their next steps. Meanwhile, Hastings asserts again how well he knows Richard, whose face he can allegedly read like a book. Having returned, Richard asks the assembled company what should be done to those who '*conspire my death with devilish plots of damned witchcraft*' (ll. 60–61). Hastings thinks they deserve death. Pointing at his crippled arm (deformed from birth as everyone present knows), Richard claims it was bewitched by Queen Elizabeth and Hastings' lover Jane Shore (formerly the king's mistress). When Hastings hesitates to confirm their guilt, Richard accuses him of treason and orders his immediate execution ('*Off with his head*', l. 76). After those who support Richard have left with him, it is Lovell and Ratcliffe's duty to take the condemned man away. Desperate, Hastings regrets neglecting the ill omens (Stanley's dream and his horse which spooked before the Tower) and realizes that Margaret's curse has come true. He predicts misery and doom for England. The fact that nobody protests against Hastings' quick condemnation shows how people, out of fear, condone a tyrant's wrongdoing and how brazen Richard's power play has become.

Examine how the theme of 'Appearance and reality' is dealt with in this scene.

Scene 5: In the courtyard of the Tower, Richard and Buckingham, dressed in armour, pretend they have to defend themselves against attackers to justify Hastings' death sentence to the Mayor of London, who is brought in by Catesby. Lovell and Ratcliffe arrive with Hastings' head and Richard insincerely mourns the man whom he took '*for the plainest harmless creature that breathed upon this earth*' (ll. 25–26). Slurring Hastings further, Buckingham claims that he plotted his and Richard's deaths, which Hastings allegedly confessed to. He then asks the Mayor to inform the general public of this, so that they do not grieve for the 'traitor' Hastings. Obviously convinced, the Mayor agrees to do so, and Richard sends Buckingham to spread malicious rumours that King Edward was an unjust and lustful man and that he and his sons are illegitimate. This slander campaign against the king's lineage is meant to move the public to be in Richard's favour when he reaches for the crown. Buckingham is to bring the Mayor and London citizens to Baynard's Castle while Lovell and Ratcliffe must summon two bishops to go there. When alone, Richard tells the audience that he will isolate the princes and Clarence's children so that nobody will have access to them.

In this scene, Richard and Buckingham speak about what it takes to be a good actor and set a scene with props and costumes for the Mayor. Outline what they thought necessary for staging a convincing performance.

Scene 6: In a monologue, a scrivener (writer of legal documents) notes that he was commissioned to write the accusation against Hastings and has finished its final form just now, when five hours ago Hastings was already charged and executed, before the document was even made public. He reflects about such gross injustice and double dealing that no one will address in the present political climate.

Point out events shown in this act which prove the correctness of the scrivener's comment on justice.

Scene 7: In Baynard's Castle, Buckingham reports to Richard that the citizens showed little enthusiasm when he tried to persuade them to see Richard as their future king. Only a few of Buckingham's followers in the back of the crowd showed their approval. Before the Mayor and the crowd arrive, Buckingham tells Richard to appear between two churchmen, as if in deep religious meditation, and to feign reluctance when responding to his requests to accept the crown. When the Mayor, the citizens and Catesby enter, Richard's henchmen pretend he is praying, much unlike the late king who was known to be a womanizer. Catesby is sent to fetch Richard and returns to say he fears harm from the crowd. When Richard finally makes an appearance on a balcony, flanked by bishops, he claims he might have displeased the Londoners, but is ready to listen to their alleged petition. Buckingham controls the crowd like a rogue politician, calling the former king '*blemished stock* (= bastard)' (l. 121) and suggesting that the remaining royal family was close to decline (ll. 127–128). Speaking as if he had the crowd's support, he urges Richard not to serve as Edward's protector, i.e. to rule in the name of the young prince, but '*to take on you the charge and kingly government of this your land*' (ll. 130–132). Displaying mock modesty, Richard replies he is unworthy of the throne which, after all, already has an heir who will surely be a good monarch. Buckingham repeats allegations of the prince being illegitimate and slanders Queen Elizabeth as a bigamist. He then exclaims that '*your brother's son shall never reign our king, but we will plant some other in the throne to the disgrace and downfall of your house*' (ll. 214–216). After Richard has restated his unwillingness to rule, the Mayor and Catesby join in with Buckingham's plea, but leave afterwards. Richard has them called back and then grudgingly agrees to accept the crown, though insisting '*how far I am from the desire thereof*' (l. 235). The citizens only ever say '*Amen*' (l. 240) during this masquerade and it is Buckingham alone who hails his co-conspirator as King Richard. The coronation is set for the following day.

Examine how Buckingham acts as Richard's strategist, mouthpiece and stage manager.

Act IV

Scene 1: Outside the Tower, Queen Elizabeth, accompanied by her son Dorset and the Duchess of York, greets Lady Anne (now Richard's wife) who entered with Clarence's daughter Margaret from a different direction. They all want to see Edward and his little brother, the Duke of York, on the prince's coronation day, but Brakenbury, the Lieutenant of the Tower, refuses them access: '*the king hath strictly charged the contrary.*' (l. 17) He amends this to 'Lord Protector', when the women protest and are outraged to be barred from visiting their family members. Stanley appears to summon Anne to her coronation in Westminster Abbey urgently. All, including Anne, are devastated to hear the news that Richard will become king. Elizabeth and Stanley press Dorset to flee to France to join Richmond, Stanley's stepson and the last remaining Lancastrian contender for the throne, whom Stanley will give notice of Dorset's arrival. Anne leaves unwillingly, remembering her curse on Richard's future wife, which has now turned against herself, and wishes to die before she becomes queen. Painfully recalling how '*my woman's heart grossly grew captive to his honey words*' (ll. 78–79), she describes the inner turmoil she has experienced at Richard's side and prophesies that he will soon kill her (ll. 80–86). In fact, this is Anne's last appearance on stage. The Duchess wishes everyone good luck, while she herself looks forward to death '*after 80 odd years of sorrow*' (l. 95). Elizabeth, who does not envy Anne becoming England's new queen, leaves for her sanctuary after bidding the Tower to treat her sons well.

Compare in what way men and women react differently to Richard's outrageous actions up to this point in the play.

Scene 2: Having finally seized the crown, Richard enters as king with all the trappings of royalty and, with Buckingham's helping hand, ascends the throne. In order to secure his kingship, he continues scheming right away. He tells Buckingham, first in veiled terms, then frankly, that he wants the princes in the Tower dead. Surprised, Buckingham hesitates and asks for time to think this over, which enrages Richard so much that he resolves not to trust him as his right-hand man any further. By order of Richard's inquiry, a page recommends a man named Tyrell as a killer who will do anything for gold, and he is then sent to fetch him. Stanley informs Richard that Elizabeth's son Dorset has fled to Richmond, Richard's enemy. Plotting more vile deeds, Richard sends Catesby to spread the rumour that Anne is '*sick and like(ly) to die*' (l. 57) and orders him to find a gentleman of low rank to marry Clarence's daughter. He believes her brother too foolish to pose a threat to his reign. In a monologue, Richard devises his plan to marry Elizabeth York, the former king's daughter, after the princes' deaths, to secure his claim to the throne. Describing his own frame of mind, he says '*I am in so far in blood that sin will pluck on* (= bring further) *sin. Tear-falling pity dwells not in this eye*' (ll. 63–65). Tyrell enters and agrees to kill friend or foe for Richard without hesitation and leaves to commit the murders for a royal favour. When Buckingham re-enters from his soul-searching, he is not given the opportunity to tell Richard what he has decided. Although Buckingham repeatedly asks for the earldom and the property he was promised, Richard refuses to grant him the reward: '*I am not in the giving vein* (= mood) *today.*' (l. 114) Richard seems distracted by the news of Dorset's flight and reminds Stanley, Richmond's stepfather, of his loyalty to him, England's new king. '*A bard of Ireland*' (l. 105) once predicted that Richard would not live long after encountering Richmond. Offended by Richard's ingratitude and change of manner as well as suddenly afraid of having to share Hastings' fate, Buckingham decides to flee '*while my fearful head is on*' (l. 120).

Assess why Richard, having become king, cannot enjoy reaching his lifelong goal, not even for a short time.
Explain Buckingham's reactions to Richard's demand and to the latter's refusal to fulfil his promise.

Scene 3: Back from his errand, Tyrell reveals in a monologue that the princes have been murdered by two hirelings. Moved by the sight of the two innocent boys and their prayer book, they could hardly carry out their orders and felt great remorse afterwards. Despite Tyrell's previously expressed lack of compassion for the victims, he calls the killings '*the most arch deed of piteous massacre that ever yet this land was* *guilty of*' (ll. 2–3). To Richard he says none of this, but simply reports the job as done and that the chaplain of the Tower has buried the boys. He leaves after Richard has promised him a reward. Richard is delighted by the fact that his plans concerning Clarence's children and his wife Anne have come to a successful result with the Plantagenet children disposed of and his queen dead. Worrying that Richmond might marry Elizabeth York before him, Richard decides to woo her without delay. When Catesby enters to inform Richard that the Bishop of Ely has fled to Richmond and Buckingham raises an army against him in Wales, Richard prepares for battle. On the one hand, Richard has consolidated his power by eliminating all other contenders for the throne and planning to marry the last Yorkist princess. On the other hand, his power diminishes at the same time as his former loyal followers, such as Buckingham and the Bishop of Ely, have turned against him.

Analyse the function of Tyrell's character in scenes 2 and 3 of this act.

Scene 4: Near the palace, Queen Margaret enters to say she has hidden in the building to watch the '*waning* (= weakening) *of mine enemies*' (l. 4) and will return to France before their final doom. When Queen Elizabeth and the Duchess of York appear, she hides from them and comments on the women's dialogue in asides. Margaret thinks it only fair that they experience losses equal to her own. Coming forward when they lament the princes' deaths, she claims an older privilege in grieving for every death in the House of Lancaster caused by the Yorkists. Regarding her own losses, the Duchess has similar complaints to make against Margaret's family. Margaret gleefully points out that Richard is to blame for the demise of his own house and reminds Elizabeth of her curse, which is now fulfilled, calling her the '*queen of sad mischance*' (l. 114). Elizabeth begs Margaret to teach her how to curse her enemy and is told that reflecting on her dead children and relatives will sharpen her tongue. After Margaret has left, the Duchess asks Elizabeth to join her in cursing her son Richard, who, at this moment, enters at the head of his army. Recalling the names of all those he had murdered, the Duchess wishes she had never born him and describes him as a devilish creature that, from his childhood, was a heavy burden on her (ll. 163–175). Richard tries to have her voice drowned out with the sound of drumming, but she tells him to listen as these are her last words to him. Cursing him and wishing success on his enemies, the Duchess promises him a shameful death in battle (ll. 184–196). Elizabeth echoes the curse and intends to leave, but Richard holds her back to speak about her daughter, also called Elizabeth. The queen begs for her daughter's life, thinking he wants her dead. In a lengthy dialogue, Richard explains that he is in love with young Elizabeth and wants to marry her, asking for her mother's advice on how to win her heart. According to him, this marriage will be advantageous to all because it secures their family's dynasty. Giving the kingdom back to her daughter and the children coming from their union will make amends for the princes' killings, of which he pronounces himself innocent, and bring peace to England. Appalled, Queen Elizabeth calls him a liar, a murderer and a usurper of the throne. Richard replies that '*death, desolation, ruin and decay*' (l. 409) will be the consequence for her family and the whole country if the marriage does not come about. Elizabeth seems to be weakening, agrees to inform the princess of Richard's plan and leaves. After she has left, he calls her a '*relenting fool, and shallow, changing woman*' (l. 431).

Ratcliffe and Catesby enter to report that a navy probably led by Richmond is approaching from the west. Richard sends Catesby to command the Duke of Norfolk to have his troops march to Salisbury. When Stanley arrives to confirm the navy are indeed Richmond's forces and that he claims the throne, Richard suspects Stanley is about to defect. Stanley denies this and promises to assemble troops for Richard's side in the north. Other opposing forces are Dorset, Buckingham and the Bishop of Ely, who are all on Richmond's side. Warning Stanley not to waver in his loyalty, Richard says he will keep Stanley's son George as a hostage and execute him if Stanley is not true to his word. Several messengers enter in quick succession to bring news of rebellions against the crown in Devon, Kent and Yorkshire. Richmond is now rumoured to have returned to France after losses at sea. Becoming more and more impatient, Richard ironically strikes the third messenger, thinking there is more bad news, but is told that Buckingham's army was scattered by flooding. Catesby re-enters and reports Buckingham's capture and Richmond's confirmed landing with mighty support in Milford Haven, Wales. Richard sets off for Salisbury with his troops and orders Buckingham to be taken there as well.

Discuss what you think of Margaret's view of justice as repayment.
A description of the relationship between mother and son is very rare in Shakespeare's plays and warm-hearted mother figures are practically non-existent. Assess in what way a mother as critical of her son as the Duchess of York might have influenced the character development of her son. Interpret Richard's reactions in his confrontation with his mother in this scene.
Comment on the nature of Richard's proposition regarding his niece, given the crimes he committed against his own family.
Discuss whether you think that Richard's arguments have persuaded Elizabeth to advocate his plan with her daughter.
This scene marks the last appearance of Queen Margaret, Queen Elizabeth and the Duchess of York in the play. Compare their exit lines and comment on the dramatic impact of their departure.
Analyse how Richard handles military matters and point out the dramatic function of the messengers' reports.

Scene 5: In his house, Stanley asks the priest Sir Christopher Urswick to assure Richmond of Stanley's whole-hearted support and to explain to him that he cannot openly send military aid because Richard holds his son, George Stanley, hostage. Urswick is told to communicate to Richmond that Queen Elizabeth has agreed to give her daughter's hand in marriage to him and not to Richard. According to Urswick, many noblemen '*of great name and worth*' (l. 16) have joined Richmond's army that has arrived in Pembroke, Wales, and is on its way to London.

Point out the forces working openly and secretly against Richard mentioned in this act.

Act V

Scene 1: On his way to his execution in Salisbury, a remorseful Buckingham reflects that All Souls' Day is a fitting day for him to die and that Richard's other victims will mock his fate from heaven. He wishes he had repented of his sins during King Edward's reign sooner and not placed his trust in Richard. Remembering Margaret's curse, he willingly goes to his death.

Discuss whether Buckingham is just a turncoat or if he truly feels regret for his actions.

Scene 2: Richmond and his troops have marched through England's midlands and are now on Tamworth plain, only a day away from Leicester, where Richard's army has taken up position. This information has reached them by a letter from Stanley, who secretly helps Richmond's cause. The Earl of Oxford, Sir James Blunt and Sir Walter Herbert have joined his ranks, and there has been no opposition so far. Richmond encourages his men to kill the '*usurping boar*' and '*foul swine*' Richard (ll. 7; 10). Everyone is confident that Richard's troops will desert him and that he will be defeated.

Very late in the play, Richmond makes his first appearance. Examine what first impression Shakespeare intended to create of his hero.

Scene 3: At sunset, King Richard, his followers, the Duke of Norfolk and the Earl of Surrey, and their army arrive at Bosworth Field near Leicester and set up their tents. Having heard that his regiment outnumbers that of his enemies three-fold, Richard is in a good mood and leaves with some men to survey the grounds and prepare for battle.

Comment on Richard's view that 'the king's name is a tower of strength' (l. 12) and will be enough motivation for his men to win the fight.

Scene 4: Having arrived with his regiment and followers at the other side of Bosworth Field, Richmond assigns power of command to each of his military leaders. He asks Captain Blunt to forward a note to Stanley, whose troops have settled half a mile to the south of Richard's forces, and withdraws with the lords to a tent to discuss their military strategy for next day's battle. Meanwhile, Richard, talking to Catesby and Ratcliffe in his tent, makes sure his armour and horse are prepared and sends a messenger to Stanley, asking him to join his army by sunrise and threatening to have Stanley's son killed if he should not arrive. Before Richard retires for the night, he comments on his lacking cheerfulness. In the meantime, Stanley has quietly stolen over to Richmond's tent, where he offers to support him in the upcoming battle by delaying the arrival of his army and explains that he could not openly fight on Richmond's side because otherwise his son would be killed. Richmond sends men to protect Stanley on his way back and, before he goes to sleep, prays to God for the well-being of his regiment and for their victory against Richard's forces.

Between the two opposing camps, a succession of ghosts arises, each the spirit of a character murdered by Richard or on his orders: Prince Edward, his father King Henry VI, Clarence, Rivers, Grey, Vaughan, Hastings, the two young princes, Anne and Buckingham. Each of them first speaks to Richard, cursing him for his misdeeds and wishing his death in battle ('*despair and die*'), and then to Richmond, whom they encourage, blessing his cause ('*live and flourish*') and prophesying Richard's defeat. Even the Yorkist ghosts promise Richmond their supernatural aid for his cause to liberate England from Richard's tyranny: '*The wrongèd heirs of York do pray for thee.*' (l. 117) When Richard wakes at midnight, he calls for '*another horse*' and thinks he was wounded in action, thereby anticipating what the oncoming battle will actually bring about. This dream leaves him deeply disturbed. He is troubled by his treachery and evil deeds and muses on the fact that nobody will pity him when he dies. His soliloquy is full of short sentences, and he jumps from one thought to another, which shows his great mental agitation. Richard's nightly visions have shaken him to such great extent that he tells Ratcliffe the '*shadows tonight*' have scared him more than 10,000 of Richmond's soldiers ever could. He also fears that some of his followers might desert him and goes to listen secretly to their conversations. A little later, at four o'clock, Richmond wakes up empowered after a good sleep, recalling the spirits wishing victory on him. He speaks to his men in an inspiring manner, pointing out that their cause is good and that God as well as '*the prayers of holy saints and wrongèd souls*' (l. 221) are on their side. He calls Richard a '*bloody tyrant and a homicide* (= murderer)' (l. 226) and '*God's enemy*' (l. 232) who must be dethroned for England's sake and tells his regiment a victorious battle will mean peace and safety for their wives and children.

Some scholars find the representation of Richard's inner turmoil after his nightmare not very convincing and difficult to play for an actor. Examine his speech and comment on the critics' view.
Discuss the effect Shakespeare might have had in mind when he created the appearance of the ghosts and what message he might have wanted to convey.

Scene 5: At his camp, Richard, Ratcliffe, Catesby and others are gathered. Richard asks for the time and if anyone has seen the sun. Thinking the black sky is a bad omen, he consoles himself by saying that it does not shine for Richmond either. Suddenly Norfolk arrives to cry for arms, and Richard hastily draws up his battle order. A mocking verse predicting their defeat has been pinned to Norfolk's tent, which Richard ignores. He then delivers a speech to his army, in which he abuses his enemies as foreign '*vagabonds, rascals, and runaways*' (l. 45) who will rape English women and are led by a weak leader untrained in battle. When Richard hears their drums, he spurs his own troops, telling them to '*ride in blood*' (l. 69). A messenger enters with the news that Stanley refuses to send his troops, whereupon Richard orders the execution of Stanley's son. Norfolk tells him to postpone this until after the battle, because Richmond's men are already approaching.

Compare Richard's and Richmond's speeches to their troops. Point out what their choice of words and arguments reveal about their personalities.

Scene 6: On the battlefield, Catesby enters to call to Norfolk for help as Richard's horse has been killed and the bravely fighting king has to continue his effort on foot. Richard appears, desperately seeking for Richmond, and says he has killed five men already whom he mistook for his archenemy. His famous cry '*A horse! A horse! My kingdom for a horse!*' (l. 13) shows what he brought upon himself by relying the fate of his crown on the outcome of a battle.

Examine Richard's behaviour in battle and what it reveals about his character.

Scene 7: Finally, the two military leaders meet and engage in hand-to-hand combat. Richmond kills Richard and the body is carried off. Triumphant, Richmond says: '*The day is ours, the bloody dog is dead.*' (l. 2) Having taken the crown from Richard's head, Stanley presents it to Richmond, saying: '*Wear it, enjoy it, and make much of it.*' (l. 7) Stanley's son George is safe in Leicester, but many nobles have been killed in action. Richmond pardons Richard's soldiers and orders to bury the dead. In his final speech he compares the state of England to a human body, which was damaged by Richard's rule ('*scarred herself*', l. 23) and has now found a '*smooth-faced peace*' (l. 33). Richmond declares the end of the civil wars (the 'Wars of the Roses') and announces his marriage to Elizabeth York, which will unite the Houses of York and Lancaster. He then prays that this will bring peace and prosperity to the country.

Comment on the overall representation of Richmond in this act and on whether he can be seen as a stereotypical force of Good needed to match and conquer the force of Evil symbolized by Richard.
Discuss why Richard undergoes such a personality change in the second half of the play and what Shakespeare's dramatic intention might have been.

The Characters

Richard

Richard (Duke of Gloucester, later King Richard III, 1452–1485) is the 'villain-hero' of this play and Shakespeare's first great creation in comparison to earlier, more ordinary characters. His spectacularly evil nature, great energy and wit make watching him quite entertaining, although he lures the audience into complicity by making them his co-conspirators. Richard's malicious joy at his own effective scheming in his monologues is shared directly with his viewers, and they might even admire his mastery of deceiving his victims. From the very beginning, when he informs the spectators of his murderous plots and characterizes himself as '*subtle, false and treacherous*' (I, i, l. 37), Richard aims for the throne unerringly, displaying a restless vitality. He is cold-blooded, feels pleasure in inflicting pain and comments humorously on his cruel deeds before or after committing them, e.g. when joking about plotting his brother Clarence's murder ('*Simple, plain Clarence, I do love thee so that I will shortly send thy soul to heaven*', I, i, ll. 118–119). Richard knows how to play on other people's greed, vanity or helplessness and uses them to do things they think they can get away with or must do to survive, on his behalf. With himself, he is brutally honest and very clear about what can give him satisfaction. As a high-ranking member of the now reigning family, he expects complete obedience and can enforce his will as he likes, e.g. when he demands the funeral procession of the former King Henry VI to stop for his sake (I, 2). His self-regard is unshakable, his disdain for others is intense and he violates moral norms by carelessly breaking any laws that might interfere with his plots. Richard lacks human virtues like gratitude, is impatient, easily enraged and incapable of love or compassion. Until the end of the play, he is in command and shows no signs of repentance.

Being king, Richard becomes even more lonely and loses some of his former supporters in his ambition to eliminate possible contenders for the throne, such as the former king's two young sons that he wants dead. When he hears of the approaching army which his sworn enemy Richmond has raised against him, he panics momentarily. Only in act V, after his nightmarish vision of his victims' ghosts who wish him defeat in battle does he truly waver for a while and reveal his inner turmoil. Nonetheless, Richard overcomes his troubled conscience quickly and resolves to stick to his unapologetic stance: '*Richard loves Richard, that is, I am I*' (V, iv, l. 163). In the end, he has totally decimated the Yorkist family with only Princess Elizabeth to continue the bloodline and has left behind nothing but destruction. When fate intervenes and Richmond ends Richard's life, the true hero of the play finally appears to restore the divine order (cf. Historical Background, p. 7). Yet, the virtuous characters working for the common good, such as Richmond and Stanley, are less interesting to observe than the cunning and duplicitous Richard who commits such horrifying deeds.

Unlike the stereotypical medieval character 'Vice', which is a personification of evil or a truly Machiavellian ruler (cf. Historical Background, pp. 14 and 17), Richard is a believable character, a human being despite his villainy, but he lacks the dignity of a tragic hero. In Shakespeare's later plays, his villains become more complex – as they are less evil than misguided, take wrong decisions, show remorse and reflect on their actions more thoroughly. All the same, Shakespeare's first archvillain continues to delight audiences and actors alike, and *Richard III* is still a popular play today.

The evil, ugly cripple

Even today, it is a common device in both literature and films to give an infamous villain a disability, e.g. Captain Hook, diverse James Bond villains or Darth Vader. Such portrayals of physical impairment in evildoers, however, convey negative images of disabled people. In Elizabethan times, it was generally thought that bodily deformities were the sign of a malicious personality, i.e. the character's inner evil manifests itself in his crippled outward appearance. In the play, Richard's particularly monstrous acts correspond to his looks of a '*bottled spider*' or '*bunch-backed toad*' (I, iii, ll. 240, 244) and many characters comment on his repulsive looks. In I, 1, Richard himself describes his unattractive exterior in frank, unflattering terms: '*rudely stamped*' (l. 16), '*curtailed of this fair proportion*' (l. 18), '*cheated of feature by dissembling nature, deformed, unfinished, sent before my time into this breathing world, scarce half made up, and that so lamely and unfashionable that dogs bark at me as I halt by them*' (ll. 19–23), '*I […] have no delight to pass away the time, unless to see my shadow in the sun and descant on* (= sing songs about) *mine own deformity*' (ll. 24–27). Though Richard says he cannot '*prove a lover*' and will therefore '*prove a villain*' (ll. 28, 30), he can turn on his charm at will and convince a mourning widow to marry him. Despite his useless arm and hunchback, Richard is a keen soldier and able swordsman. Besides, he is also supremely self-confident, has charisma and is very intelligent. Modern psychology might see his family's reaction to his physique as a contributing factor in or reason for Richard's compensatory strategies and his punishment for them. An assessment of his character traits would probably conclude with a diagnosis of him being an arrogant and narcissistic sociopath as well as a pathological liar with a compulsive desire to dominate, who has no remorse, conscience or guilt.

The brilliant actor

Richard is a gifted deceiver and smooth talker who can fool others into completely believing what he claims, e.g. when

- pretending to be a loyal follower of his brother, King Edward IV, (II, 1) and a loving uncle and protector of his children (III, 1),
- convincing his brother Clarence of his heartfelt wish to help with the latter's cause when he is arrested and taken to prison, suggesting it is Queen Elizabeth's fault and not Richard's very own that Clarence is suspected of treason in I, 1,
- playing the role of a lover when wooing Lady Anne and pretending to have killed her husband for love for her (I, 2),
- putting on a show to ask for his mother's blessing in II, 2,
- staging an imaginary defence against attacking enemies with Buckingham to justify the execution of Hastings in III, 5,
- presenting himself as a deeply honest and religious man in front of the mayor and citizens and feigning reluctance to accept the crown after the princes have been declared 'illegitimate' in III, 7.

Richard's relationships

Richard III is Richard's play, which he dominates by the sheer amount of stage time he has – he speaks one-third of the lines and all major soliloquies. Until his downfall, he manoeuvres all others around and is in constant interaction with them, often mocking or insulting them.

Even when he is not on stage, he is ever-present in the other characters' minds, who talk about him or wonder what he might do next and thus constantly draw attention to him. As no tyrant operates in a vacuum, the other characters are mainly shown in their respective attitude towards him. Some are followers, such as Buckingham or Hastings, who know how vicious Richard is, but want to profit personally by staying close to him or helping to do his dirty work. Ironically, they are among the first ones he gets rid of. Others, such as James Tyrell or the assassins, are ready to do any of Richard's bidding, including unlawful or immoral acts like murder, without further ado. In the political climate after King Edward IV's death, some characters feel insecure about the country's fate and also worry about their own fates if they take any wrong decisions and therefore condone Richard's actions. They are also unaware of Richard's plots and frightened by his threats, e.g. the royal women. Others are fooled by him, e.g. Clarence, the London mayor and citizens or the royal children, and naively accept or want to believe what Richard told them.

How historians see Richard

Modern scholars see the historical Richard as innocent of most crimes attributed to him and as no better or worse than other English kings. It is known that some of his supposed victims in the play, such as Lady Anne's fiancé Prince Edward or Clarence, either died in battle or were killed by other people's orders. There is even speculation that Richmond, who succeeded to Richard's throne as King Henry VII, might have ordered the unsolved murders of the two young princes to secure his position. Richard seized the throne after the death of his brother, King Edward IV, as a consequence of Queen Elizabeth and her family's two coups to crown the young Prince of Wales quickly, although a royal child had to be represented by a regent or Lord Protector. In 1483, Richard took the crown himself, under circumstances that cannot be reconstructed, and reigned for merely two years. An assessment of how successful or competent he was as a king remains impossible.

Shakespeare's portrait of Richard as an evil monster shaped the public imagination. There is even an organization which seeks to clear his name posthumously, the *Richard III Society* founded in 1924. In Tudor paintings, the historical Richard is shown as having a crippled arm and a hunchback, and for a long time scholars believed this to be a misrepresentation due to the propaganda of the 'Tudor Myth' (cf. Historical Background, pp. 12–13). In 2012, Richard's remains were found under a car park in Leicester, where he is supposed to have been buried in a church-like building next to the battlefield where he died. His bones show a curvature in his spine that confirms his depiction in contemporary portraits. Richard was reburied with pomp in Leicester Cathedral in 2015.

King Edward IV

At the beginning of the play, Richard's oldest brother Edward (1442–1483) has just ascended the throne after the Yorkist victory over the Lancastrians. However, he is seriously ill and is seen on stage only in II, 1, when he learns of his brother Clarence's death. It is implied that the misery this information causes him leads to his own demise which is reported in II, 2. Richard has called Clarence's trustworthiness into question and spread the rumour that Clarence poses a threat to Edward's children. Although King Edward had earlier ordered Clarence's imprisonment and execution for treason, he has reversed the sentence. Edward has two sons with Queen Elizabeth, who are the heirs to his throne and are later murdered by Richard, and a daughter King Richard plans to marry in order to secure his crown. The historical Edward IV reigned for 22 years and was known for his overindulgence in wine and women (there is a reference to his mistress Jane Shore in I, i, l. 73), which might have contributed to his early death. Shakespeare's portrayal of his kingship is therefore extremely unhistorical, because, in the play, he dies shortly after his coronation.

The Duke of Clarence

Richard's and Edward's middle brother George (1449–1478, always called 'Clarence') is a good-hearted and trusting man. He shifted his loyalty from the York family to the Lancastrians before the play begins, because he disapproved of Edward's wife Elizabeth, a commoner,

The Houses of York and Lancaster, and the Foundation of the Tudor Dynasty

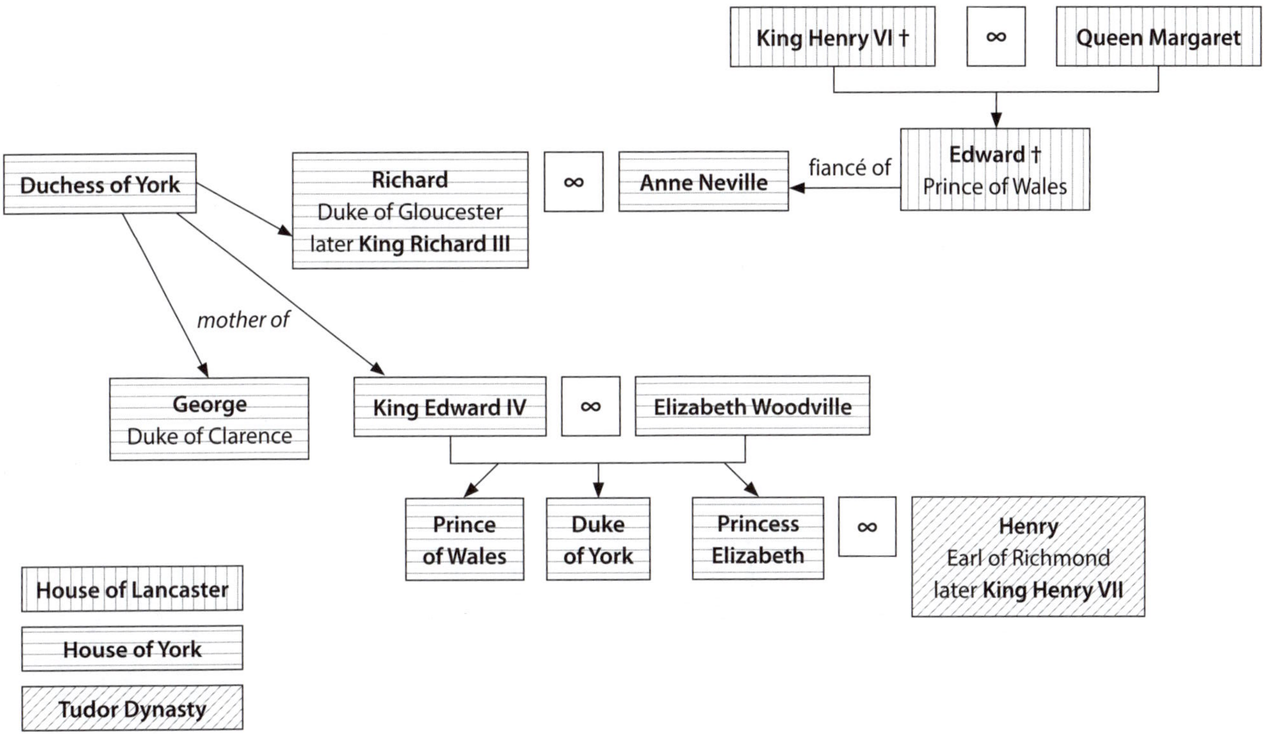

whom he could not imagine a good queen. At this point in the story, Clarence is reconciled with King Edward, but their strained relations explain why the king believes the prophecy invented by Richard that Clarence might be his downfall. He only appears in two scenes: In I, 1, Clarence is under arrest and on his way to the Tower, while I, 4 shows him in his cell, waking after a nightmare before two murderers sent by Richard arrive and stab him to death. Offstage, he is put into a cask of wine to ensure that he is dead. Clarence's prophetic dream of danger coming from his brother does not make him suspicious, however, and he cannot believe the murderers' claim that they have their orders from Richard. He movingly begs them to reconsider, lamenting his fate, and manages to convince one of his killers of the wrongness of their murderous intentions. Historically, Richard protested against his brother's imprisonment and it was King Edward IV who, after forgiving Clarence several times for plotting against him in the Wars of the Roses, finally sentenced him to death.

Shakespeare uses Clarence as a foil for Richard, contrasting his remorse about his part in the wars with Richard's revelling in his deeds, and his good nature and decency with Richard's malice.

The Duchess of York

Her three sons, King Edward IV, the Duke of Clarence and Richard, the Duke of Gloucester, are celebrating their victory over the Lancastrian forces at the beginning of the play. The Duchess of York (Cicely Neville, 1415–1485) actually hates the evil nature of her son Richard, who has made her life painful, starting with his birth (IV, iv, ll. 166–175). After his coronation, she thinks him responsible for the death of her other two sons and grandsons and wishes him to die '*by God's just ordinance* (= order)' (IV, iv, l. 184) in the battle to come, disowning and cursing him roundly like Queen Margaret before her and thus reinforcing the criticism of Richard's deeds. She also must endure her son's insinuation that she has been unfaithful to her husband and that her son King Edward was illegitimate, which would make his direct successors unfit for the crown. Shakespeare's sources (cf. Historical Background, p. 18) hardly mention her, and many critics think that her function as a symbolic figure is similar to that of the chorus in ancient Greek drama which does not participate in the action but comments on it from the outside and warns of forthcoming events. Considering that she is his mother, the catalogue of Richard's faults and her death wish for him are particularly striking.

Queen Elizabeth

The wife of King Edward IV, Elizabeth Woodville (1437–1492), is hated by the old nobility because she was a commoner, a poor widow with children when the king married her and thus brought her into aristocratic ranks. She used her royal status to promote her relatives to high-ranking positions or to organize marriages to rich heiresses. Her children with King Edward will be his successors and she worries greatly about their fates once her sick husband dies. Queen Elizabeth is rightly suspicious of Richard when he becomes the Lord Protector for her oldest son, Prince Edward, until he can reign alone. She flees to a sanctuary and has her sons taken away from her. Elizabeth must suffer the executions of Lord Grey, her son by her previous husband, and that of her brother Lord Rivers as well as the disappearance of both her young sons by Edward in the Tower of London, then a prison. She manages to persuade the remaining older son of her first marriage, the Marquess of Dorset, to escape from England. Horrified by Richard's proposal to marry her daughter, also Elizabeth, the queen deceives him into believing that she accepts this, although she has secretly allied herself with the Earl of Richmond, Richard's enemy, before his invasion of England and has already promised him her daughter. Queen Elizabeth is tougher than Lady Anne, but not very strong, and bravely takes on the blows fate holds ready for her. She suffers throughout the play and seeks comfort in the company of the other women. Though haunted by Queen Margaret's curse, she still wants the old woman to teach her such condemnations to heap on Richard. The historical Elizabeth Woodville lived out her life at the court of her son-in-law Richmond, then King Henry VII.

The royal children

King Edward IV's and Queen Elizabeth's children, Edward Prince of Wales, Richard Duke of York and Princess Elizabeth, have become fair game for Richard after their father's death. As their Lord Protector, he sends the princes to the Tower, allegedly for their own safety, where he has them killed by James Tyrell's henchmen. Richard proposes to Queen Elizabeth that he will marry the princess, which she pretends to accept, although she has already promised her to Richmond. In order to protect his throne, Richard imprisons Clarence's son Edward Plantagenet, and marries his daughter Margaret Plantagenet off to a man of low rank. Historically, the mystery of who ordered the princes' murders that Tyrell confessed to in 1502 remains unsolved, and scholars believe that both Richard as well as Richmond had a shaky claim to the throne that might have induced them to plot this atrocity.

Queen Margaret

Queen Margaret (Margaret of Anjou, 1430–1482) is the French-born widow of Lancastrian King Henry VI, whose life and politics are described in Shakespeare's plays *Henry VI*, parts 1, 2 and 3. In these plays, Margaret is portrayed as a scheming, courageous, but also cruel military leader. Her final appearance in *Richard III* shows her as a personification of revenge or retribution. Here, she is half insane with grief and mourns for her dead husband and her son Edward, Lady Anne's husband, to such an extent that her hatred seems to be the only thing that keeps her alive. She has returned from her exile in France to observe those who are now in power, reminds them of past grievances and curses all of them elaborately. Disregarding her own crimes (shown in the *Henry* plays), she wants the family, who profited in the Wars of the Roses, to suffer or be destroyed and predicts their downfall or deaths. When Queen Elizabeth shares Margaret's fate of losing her loved ones, the old queen gloats over her misfortunes. Content to have seen the misery of the family responsible for the decline of her own family, Margaret leaves England for France before the climax of the play and Richard's death. Several characters ruefully mention her prophecies before their own deaths.

The historical Margaret was not as influential or warrior-like as suggested by Shakespeare and did not witness her son's death as the play's character claims. Her appearance in *Richard III* takes place at a time when the real Margaret had already died. Shakespeare has used her as a witchlike figure from foreign shores who embodies evil and vengeance. Like the Duchess of York, scholars have compared Margaret's function in the play to that of the chorus in ancient Greek drama.

Lady Anne

In England's civic strife, Richard helped kill the husband of Lady Anne (Anne Neville, later Richard's Queen Anne, 1456–1485), Prince Edward of Wales, and his father Henry VI. While following her father-in-law's coffin, she is approached and courted by Richard in I, 2. Initially repulsed, she curses him for his actions, but is nevertheless mesmerized by the claim that he killed the two men only because of her beauty. Being too weak and unable to stab Richard in retaliation for his crimes with the knife he has given her, she finally accepts the ring he offers her and later also his marriage proposal. Lady Anne returns as Richard's wife, the Duchess of Gloucester, in IV, 1 and says she would rather die than become queen (ll. 57–62). She correctly foresees that she will be his next victim. When rumour has it that she has fallen sick, it is implied that Richard has killed her, too.

Historically, Lady Anne did not attend King Henry's funeral, and she was only engaged to marry the prince. She married Richard in 1474 and most likely died of natural causes. There was a solar eclipse on the day of her death, which many might have seen as a bad omen for Richard's kingship.

The women

All mourning women meet to talk about their loss of loved ones and the horrors of their lives, which were mostly caused by Richard. They belong to different generations, but they have suffered a similar fate at Richard's hands, are united in their hatred of him and lament that they have become his victims. The strength of their emotions differs, and some are less helpless than others, but ultimately their position in society determines their roles that cow them into submission. Much unlike Shakespeare's contemporary ruler, Queen Elizabeth I, these women could not wield any power and are only allowed declamation. However, they are emotionally strong and speak a powerful language, especially in their curses of Richard. Their function is to show the impact the men's actions have on the people and the country and to move the audience to compassion, which Richard's attempts at silencing them cannot prevent.

Richard's view of women is misogynistic and contemptuous, which he expresses ruthlessly, e.g.: '*Was ever woman in this humour wooed? Was ever woman in this humour won? I'll have her, but I will not keep her long.*' (about Lady Anne, I, ii, ll. 224–226) or '*Relenting fool, and shallow, changing woman*' (about Queen Elizabeth, IV, iv, l. 431).

The Duke of Buckingham

The Duke of Buckingham (Henry Stafford, 1455–1483) is Richard's most powerful and conspiratorial strategist before he turns away from him because of the king's ingratitude. He is unsure about the political developments after King Edward's death and has an eye for opportunities but does not come forward to recommend himself for any position. Buckingham is a diplomat who is sent by Edward to make peace between the Yorkist brothers in I, 3, and he is the only one not cursed by old Queen Margaret. Ambitious and ruthless, Buckingham thinks Richard the most likely candidate to succeed in the power vacuum after Edward's death and becomes his right-hand man, e.g. when they hatch the plot against Hastings in III, 4, or when the young princes are sent to the Tower for safe-keeping (III, 1). Despite their seemingly close relationship, Richard thinks little of Buckingham and calls him a '*simple gull*' (I, iii, l. 326). Richard promises him a vast fortune and the earldom of Hereford if he helps to persuade the citizens of London and the mayor that Richard should be the next king (III, 5). However, when Richard wants Buckingham to kill the young princes, he hesitates and leaves to think this over. Meanwhile, Richard has found a willing assassin and dismisses Buckingham, who does not answer whether he is ready to kill the princes or not. Richard reacts angrily, when Buckingham reminds him of the earldom he was promised. Realizing that Richard will never grant this, Buckingham collects troops to rebel against the king, but is prevented to march by a storm. He is taken prisoner and acknowledges his own guilt frankly before he is executed in V, 1.

According to historians, the duke was one of the most powerful men in the country, a man the king would have wanted on his side. The reasons for his revolt are not known, but it is not the one Shakespeare gives him, because the actual Richard gave Buckingham his earldom before he decided to oppose the king.

The Earl of Richmond

Henry Tudor (Earl of Richmond, later King Henry VII, 1457–1509) is the last surviving Lancastrian male, having fled England after the Yorkists had won the last battle in the war of the two Houses. He is the hero-figure who arrives only in V, 2, though his army's advance from France is noted with panic by Richard in Act IV. In the night before the Battle of Bosworth the ghosts of Richard's victims wish victory on Richmond and he wins the combat by defeating Richard in a sword-fight. The Earl of Richmond is energetic, God-fearing and filled with his mission to overthrow Richard and to fight for the good of his country. In the medieval Morality Plays (cf. Historical Background, p. 17), he would embody the Force of Good that finally beats the Evil represented by Richard. Richmond acts as a redeemer for the crimes and sins both branches of the Plantagenet family have committed. He ends their conflict when uniting the Houses of York and Lancaster by his marriage to the Yorkist princess Elizabeth and ruling as King Henry VII, as the first Tudor monarch.

The historical Richmond was a successful ruler who brought peace and reconciliation to his country but was a ruthless king when it came to securing his reign against enemies. In order to influence the public's view of his seizure of power, he encouraged the blackening of Richard III's character (the 'Tudor Myth', cf. Historical Background, pp. 12–13).

Lord William Hastings

In prison when the play opens and having fallen from favour through Queen Elizabeth's and her relatives' influence, Lord Hastings (~ 1430–1483) loyally supports Richard when he is released. He never doubts Gloucester's sincerity and is thus easily deceived. Hastings profits from Richard's rise to power but is the first who refuses to assist him in his attempt to seize the crown from its rightful heirs. Lacking imagination and judgement of character, Hastings does not comprehend that his situation has changed due to this decision and he ignores all warnings and omens that point at Richard's guilt. In a sudden move in III, 4, Richard fabricates an accusation of treason against him and immediately sentences him to death. The historical Hastings took part in an attempt to remove Richard from his position as Lord Protector of the young prince and was subsequently executed without a trial.

Lord Thomas Stanley

Lord Stanley (Earl of Derby, ~1435–1504) secretly supports his stepson Richmond's invasion, although he promises military support to Richard. Throughout the play, he is careful not to reveal his true feelings, which become apparent when he warns Hastings and advises Queen Elizabeth's son Dorset to join Richard's enemy in France. Since Richard suspects him to feign loyalty, he takes Stanley's son George as a hostage and threatens to kill him if Stanley is not true to his word. However, Stanley allies himself with Richmond at Bosworth Field before the battle begins. Richard orders George Stanley's execution, but it is not carried out. After Richard dies in combat, Stanley presents the crown to Richmond, while he is still on the battlefield.

Minor characters

- Also called flat characters or stereotypes, minor characters have few qualities and do not undergo a development during the play.
- They do not appear very frequently and often only have a function for a particular scene, such as the Lieutenant of the Tower, Brakenbury, who allows Clarence's murderers to enter his cell, thereby showing that he does not dare question Richard's orders, or the ghosts of King Henry VI and his son, who do not appear in the play other than as spirits to wish Richard ill luck in the battle to come.
- Sometimes they are only referred to and are not present on stage, such as King Edward's mistress Jane Shore and Princess Elizabeth, his daughter.
- Minor characters have a particular purpose in the play, e.g. to:
  - mirror a main character or serve as a foil for him or her, such as King Edward and Clarence whose human qualities are contrasted with Richard's malevolence, or Lady Anne, whose fate and unhappiness mirrors that of the other royal women,
  - fill the stage to represent a court or society, such as the churchmen, the Mayor of London, the citizens, or as followers of one faction, such as Richard's followers Catesby, Norfolk or Ratcliffe or Richmond's allies Oxford, Blunt and Herbert or the Woodville family with Rivers, Grey and Vaughan,
  - add to the atmosphere of the place and carry out their work or profession, such as servants, messengers, scriveners, soldiers or murderers.

Themes

Appearance and reality

In many plays, the theme of what is real and what only seems to be real is the focus of the dramatist's intention. Sometimes characters misinterpret circumstances or other characters or lack the essential information to get a full picture of the situation. When the truth about matters is finally revealed, the characters usually learn the lesson not to take everything for granted or trust others unquestioningly. In this play, Shakespeare's intention is to warn against deceivers and their unethical schemes. In *Richard III*, it is the titular character's wilful deception that, together with Buckingham's assistance, fools almost every one of the characters until the very end. From the start, the audience is aware of Richard's intrigues and watches him weave his web around his victims: '*Plots have I laid*' (I, i, l. 32). Proud of his own acting talent, he describes how he will play the God-fearing man nobody suspects of treachery: '*But then I sigh, and with a piece of scripture tell them that God bids us do good for evil. And thus I clothe my naked villainy with odd old ends stol'n forth of holy writ* (= the Bible), *and seem a saint, when most I play the devil.*' (I, iii, ll. 332–336) Buckingham is equally sure of being a great performer when he boasts: '*I can counterfeit* (= imitate) *the deep tragedian, speak and look back, and pry on every side, tremble and start at wagging* (= shaking) *of a straw, intending deep suspicion. Ghastly looks are at my service, like enforcèd smiles, and both are ready in their offices* (= at my command), *at any time to grace my stratagems* (= clever plans).' (III, v, ll. 5–11) In III, 7, their masterpiece of stagecraft is presented to the London Mayor and citizens, who do not see through their hypocritical charade of introducing a reluctant candidate for the crown.

Clarence cannot believe his brother wants him dead, and his prophetic dream shows him drowning due to Richard's actions – a fate that actually awaits him shortly afterwards. Hastings realizes Richard's duplicity only when it is too late, and the other lords present do not dare to point out the falsehood of Richard's accusation about Hastings having shrunk Richard's arm by witchcraft, although everybody knows he was born with it. Some characters, such as Queen Elizabeth or Stanley, are distrustful of Richard, but cannot know the full extent of his falsehood and must pay the ultimate price of losing family members.

Betrayal

In *Richard III*, particular attention is drawn to deceit – nobody is excepted from treachery. Richard betrays others and they, too, already have or will betray him as part of the power politics the York and Lancaster families are involved in. Richard and his henchman Buckingham deceive others to achieve the crown in the first three acts of the play. They spread rumours about their enemies and Richard hires assassins to get rid of those who are in his way. Although Buckingham is Richard's confidant and can judge how treacherous Gloucester is, he is surprised by Richard's refusal to grant him the promised reward for his efforts. Alone, Richard constantly uses subtle tactics, acting skills and persuasive language to sway people, e.g. Clarence or Lady Anne (I, 1 and 2). Ironically, it seems to be a child that hints at a possible betrayal by Richard, when Prince Edward, the heir to the throne, is about to be sent to the Tower 'for his own safety'. His younger brother fears that the ghost of their uncle Clarence will haunt the place, whereas Edward says: '*I fear no uncles dead. […] And if they live, I hope I need not fear.*' (III, i, ll. 147–148) To bring about Richard's downfall, Queen Elizabeth and Stanley need to betray Richard in order to assist Richmond in his uprising against the usurper. Sharing their great misery, the Duchess of York, Lady Anne and the queen with her children are the only ones who do not betray each other.

Justice and punishment

Much like in a 'Morality Play', all sinners get their punishments, even for crimes that date back to past events which are not shown in this last sequel of Shakespeare's history plays. Elizabethan theatre-goers expected divine justice to be restored and punishment to be meted out to the characters who deserved it, especially to usurpers who upset the hierarchical order of the concept of the *Chain of Being* that saw the king as God's representative on earth (cf. Historical Background, p. 7). Richard's list of victims consists of 11 characters, and he claims to have personally killed the former King Henry VI and his son Edward before the play begins. Executions are either ordered by him to remove heirs to the throne (Clarence, his two nephews), to punish treason (Hastings, Buckingham) or to weaken Queen Elizabeth's family (Rivers, Grey, Vaughan). Lady Anne dies of mysterious causes, but since Richard has had the news made public that she is sick and likely to die, he will have been responsible for her demise as well. It is Richard who causes King Edward IV's rapid decline in health and his death, when he announces that, contrary to the king's decision, their brother Clarence has been killed. By the end of the play, Richard has almost wiped out both dynasties completely. Some scholars have suggested that his kingship itself is God's punishment for the war the Houses of York and Lancaster have waged with each other. In this view, by killing Richard and beginning a new dynasty, Richmond, like a divine redeemer, delivers England from her state of calamity and brings peace to the country.

Family conflict

In what was later called the 'Wars of the Roses' (1455–1487), the two branches of the Plantagenet dynasty fiercely battled each other to win the crown. If not always related by blood, they were connected by their noble background or common history and were actively engaged in political affairs. Within the royal family, there is also the controversy between the true Yorkists and Queen Elizabeth's relatives, the Woodvilles. Every character in *Richard III* has a long-standing relationship with every other character and their mutual treatment is one of backstabbing, treachery and bloodshed. They often accuse each other, citing the other families' brutal acts, and all suffer the consequences of their intense violence. Excepting the children, none of them is innocent with Richard being the devil incarnate who even ruthlessly orders the deaths of his brother Clarence and his nephews. The few characters who try to reconcile the quarrelling parties, such as Clarence and King Edward, meet their untimely ends already in the first act and cannot exert any positive influence on their family.

Performance History and Criticism

Little is known about the early productions of *Richard III*, one of Shakespeare's earliest plays and the second-longest after *Hamlet*. It was probably written between 1591 and 1593 and its first recorded performance at the royal court took place in 1633. However, in 1593 a play called *Buckingham*, which could have been *Richard III*, was referenced by Philip Henslowe, a London theatrical manager. The fact that *Richard III* was published in several separate editions ('Quartos') in the late 16th and early 17th centuries also suggests that it was frequently performed on stage. There are a bookseller's description and other contemporary references to the play's notorious villain, suggesting that Richard was a popular stage character well before the 1630s.

In the Restoration period (1660–1689) and up to the 18th century, it was common to adapt, cut or even change scenes or endings to suit the times. Colley Cibber's starkly trimmed version of the play (1700), which was to remain popular for about 150 years, was the first Shakespearean play to be staged in America (New York, 1751). Cibber eliminated several major characters, such as Edward IV, Clarence and Queen Margaret, and focused wholly on the protagonist, adding large sections he had written himself, like the onstage murder of the princes.

Famous for his naturalistic acting, David Garrick (1717–1779) adopted the role he played for more than thirty years. Edmund Kean (1787–1833) favoured highly charged acting and enjoyed the richly different aspects of Richard's character. Shakespeare's original version was brought back on stage in the 1870s by Britain's greatest actor of the Victorian stage, Henry Irving (1838–1905), who called Richard one of his four favourite roles in his long acting career. From this time on, the play has always been cut extensively because of its length.

During Germany's fascist era, directors of *Richard III* have compared the main character to Adolf Hitler, an interpretation later echoed by the National Theatre stage performance in 1990 and in a following film version with Ian McKellen as a dictator-like Richard (director: Richard Loncraine, 1995).

In the 20th and 21st centuries, the play's sinister villain has been played by famous British actors on stage and screen, such as Laurence Olivier (in a film in which Margaret's part was omitted, 1955), Ian

Holm (Royal Shakespeare Company, 1963) or Kathryn Hunter (Shakespeare's Globe, 2003). In an all-female production, Hunter's Richard reminded the audience of a monkey whose crippled fingers the courtiers had to kiss, while Kevin Spacey in a production at the Old Vic Theatre (2011) emphasized the protagonist's deformity with leg braces. Referring to Queen Margaret's description of Richard as a 'bottled spider', Antony Sher played Richard on crutches in a Royal Shakespeare Company production in 1984. Dressed all in black, the 'added legs' gave him the grotesque appearance of a large spider or cockroach. Richard's archetype is reflected in the TV series *House of Cards*, in which a senior politician uses comparable strategies to become the prime minister or president of his country (original BBC production, 1990–95; American Netflix version, 2013–18). Just like the play's protagonist plays to the audience directly, breaking the 'fourth wall', on TV, Francis Urquhart/Underwood looks right into the camera when explaining his diabolical plans. In more than 400 years on stage, Richard has remained one of Shakespeare's most popular characters and the play is continually reinterpreted and performed all over the world.

Up to the 20th century, traditional criticism of *Richard III*, seeing the play as a tragedy and not as a history play, has adopted the Aristotelian definition of a tragic hero whose fate is inescapable, as he has greatly sinned. He must suffer and finally be killed for the crimes he has committed, after which harmony and hope can reign again. Although Richard undoubtedly is a villain and not a hero, like in a tragedy, the rise and fall of a high-ranking character is portrayed, and the First Folio of 1623, the first collection of Shakespeare's plays in printed form, describes the play on its title page as *The Tragedy of Richard the Third*. Critics of this school have concentrated on the study of the characters and treated them as if they were real human beings. They considered the hero afflicted with a tragic flaw, in this case his ambition to be king, which mainly caused the tragedy. This "character criticism" does not include any social, economic, historical or political factors which are dealt with in modern critical approaches.

In the first half of the 20th century, different critics saw Shakespeare's plays as explorations of important themes (e.g. the conflict between appearance and reality or justice and punishment), as having image-clusters as a dominant feature (e.g. evil vs. good imagery) or thought the plays should be studied for their poetic language or their stagecraft. Critical approaches to Shakespeare's plays were radically transformed in the last quarter of the 20th century, when modern criticism focused on singular viewpoints, often opposed to each other.

Taking the historical conditions into account, political criticism sees the characters as determined by their circumstances and the society they lived in. Viewed from this standpoint, James Tyrell and the other murderers would be both the victims and the enforcers of a corrupt society. The characters involved in the Wars of the Roses are all descendants of the Plantagenet dynasty and its two branches, the York and the Lancaster families. Historically, their violent struggle for the crown began when a weak king, Richard II, was deposed by the Lancastrian Henry Bolingbroke in 1399 and the Yorkists fought to gain the political leadership. Political criticism would thus see their infighting not as an attempt to restore a divine order, but as driven by self-interest. In this scenario, religion does not play a major role, but gives way to political pressure and social realities.

Psychological criticism, influenced by Sigmund Freud's theories, highlights the characters' unconscious and irrational desires, fears and sexuality. It cannot be proved, though, that there is a 'hidden content' behind the 'manifest content' of the text or play itself, as this approach suggests. Among other issues, psychoanalysis is concerned with the disruption of family relationships, which is at the heart of this play. Therefore, Richard's motivations for his plotting and the way he is treated by others are of interest. His own mother launches a tirade of abuse against him which culminates in her reproach '*Thou cam'st on earth to make my earth my hell*' (IV, iv, l. 167). He himself bitterly describes his deformities in his first monologue (I, 1) and other people's negative reactions to him are made obvious throughout the play, so that critics of this school of thought might argue that Richard treats people abominably as a consequence of the apparent disgust they have felt for him. Not having been loved, Richard is unable to feel or give love and capable of committing his terrible atrocities because he has never learned to experience empathy. His success in charming Lady Anne is not due to his sexual passion, but to his theatrical talent of playing the ardent lover. Besides, one could say that a mother who is full of hatred for her son will probably have evoked the strong feeling of misogyny in Richard he so often expresses.

Pointing out how female experience is shown or how pervasive patriarchal ideas are, feminist criticism or gender studies challenge sexism. In the medieval world portrayed in the play, women are the victims of the vicious main character, who hates women with sadistic pleasure and enjoys deceiving his female counterparts and letting the viewers know how much contempt he feels for them. There was no chance for a widowed queen to keep her power, and all Elizabeth could do to safeguard her son's claim to the throne was to hasten his ascension to the throne and avoid Richard's rule as a Lord Protector. Having failed at this, she can only flee to a sanctuary and try to save her sons, which is also prevented by Gloucester. Elizabeth can save her daughter from a marriage to Richard, but the girl is a pawn in the political power play and has no say in the matter. Even as the last remaining royal child, the princess cannot become the country's ruler, as only male descendants can inherit the crown. The three noblewomen Elizabeth, Anne and the Duchess of York are shown in IV, 1 as a kind of sisterhood that sympathizes with the others' worries, as well as later with Margaret in IV, 4, when they mourn their respective losses. Margaret is less sympathetic, since she also berates Elizabeth for her role in their past history. Together with the Duchess, Elizabeth curses Richard, claiming the moral high ground. Though the women's active influence is restricted, they possess strong emotive power and succeed in conveying the deep feelings of grief Richard's crimes have created.

Adaptations and Spin-offs

Shakespeare's dramatic story of one man's ambition, deception and murderous nature has inspired adaptations throughout the centuries in literature, film, music and popular culture. They are worthwhile studying to see how differently the play and its themes can be interpreted or which focus the respective artists found most interesting. The most important film versions are:

Richard III in films

Richard III, recorded on stage at the Shakespeare Memorial Theatre in Stratford-upon-Avon, 1911.
A black and white silent film (22') showing several tableaux with quotes from the play.

Richard III, director and male lead Laurence Olivier, 1955.
Olivier's interpretation of the role was long seen as 'definitive', though his acting style is considered dated today.

Richard III, director Richard Loncraine, 1995, with Ian McKellen as Richard, who also wrote the screenplay after playing Richard on stage for the National Theatre in 1990.
The setting is an imaginary 1930s England with Richard using fascist methods to rise to power. In the short film *Shooting Shakespeare: Richard III* (25', The Film Space on Vimeo) McKellen, Loncraine and academics discuss aspects of the play and its filming.

Richard III, director Dominic Cooke, 2016, with Benedict Cumberbatch as Richard as final part of the BBC TV series *The Hollow Crown – The Wars of the Roses*, a film version of the first tetralogy.

Examinations of *Richard III*

Al Pacino's documentary film *Looking for Richard* (1996) contains some scenes with Pacino playing Richard and discussions with actors and academics about characters and themes.
Richard III with Sir Antony Sher (2018) is part of the PBS series 'Shakespeare Uncovered', in which Sher, who has played Richard in the Royal Shakespeare Company staging of the play (1984), examines the role and the historical Richard.

Spin-offs

Michael Dobbs' novels *House of Cards* (1989), *To Play the King* (1993) and *The Final Cut* (1995) were dramatized for a BBC TV trilogy (1990–1995) and for an American Netflix version (2013–2018). The protagonists Francis Urquhart / Underwood are corrupt politicians aiming for the positions of British Prime Minister / US President and draw from Richard, since they are as unscrupulous and murderous as Shakespeare's villain.

Language, Style and Dramatic Devices

Language and style

The basic formal pattern of regular ***blank verse*** (unrhymed verse with 10 to 11 syllables per line) is typical of Shakespeare's early plays. Later in his career, his characters speak using run-on-lines, in which they express an idea or describe situations in several lines. In *Richard III*, lines often stop with a punctuation mark and contain a statement complete in itself, although more sentence parts might follow until the final full stop. Only occasionally does Shakespeare deviate from the usual rhythm in order to show e.g. his characters' agitation, which is expressed in broken sentences or exclamations. In V, 4, after Richard's nightmare before the Battle of Bosworth, the usually measured rhythm breaks into fragments in order to portray Richard's emotional upset and loss of control. When he regains his composure and decides to follow his envisioned path, the interrupted meter – '*Richard loves Richard, that is, I am I*' (l. 163) – underlines the strength of his will power. Unlike the plays that follow, *Richard III* is written almost entirely in verse. Generally, only the characters from lower classes speak in prose, such as the two murderers of Clarence in I, 4.

Shakespeare lets Richard reveal his true feelings and innermost thoughts in ***soliloquies*** (= monologues), which he confides exclusively to the audience, making them the unwilling co-conspirators of his designs. By talking directly to the audience (= breaking the "fourth wall"), characters establish a strong connection and create suspense regarding their intended actions.

Figures of speech, imagery and symbols

In his early plays, Shakespeare often uses many stylistic devices in an almost formal way, as if he wanted to show his rhetorical skills. By this, he heightens the dramatic effect of a scene and intensifies the emotional expressions of the characters. For instance, he models the rapid exchanges of single lines between Richard and Queen Elizabeth on a Greek figure of speech called *stichomythia* (IV, iv, ll. 212–218; 343–367; 418–430), thereby creating the impression of a quick sparring fight between two equally eloquent contestants. Occasionally, they even have their war of words only in half lines (IV, iv, ll. 267–271; 374–377). Another figure of speech called *asteismus* can be found when both Richard and Queen Elizabeth use the words 'soul' and 'love' with an unexpected ironical twist after Richard has proclaimed that '*from my soul I love thy daughter*' (IV, iv, ll. 256–263).

In the following, here are some examples of the many instances of Shakespeare's rhetorical devices:

- *Anaphora* – the repetition of words or phrases at the beginning of clauses for emphasis
  Richard's use of 'our' in I, I, ll. 5–8, or Margaret's 'for' in IV, iv, ll. 98–104
- *Antithesis* – the opposition of words or phrases, e.g. to illustrate a conflict
  Richard: '*And if King Edward be as true and just as I am subtle, false and treacherous*' (I, i, ll. 36–37) or the Duchess of York lamenting her grandson's death: '*Dead life, blind sight, poor mortal living ghost*' (IV, iv, l. 26). Anne on a fitting place for Richard: '*Some dungeon.*' His suggestion: '*Your bedchamber.*' (I, ii, ll. 111–112).
- *List* – the enumeration of several things in order to intensify description or atmosphere
  In IV, iv, ll. 167–175, Richard's mother lists the many ways in which, since his birth, he has made her life miserable. Richard and Buckingham enumerate the different aspects of an actor's craft in III, v, ll. 1–11.
- *Metaphor* – a comparison that is only implied, ascribing qualities of one thing to another
  Richard describes the past troubles as '*winter*' and '*clouds that loured upon* (= threatened) *our house*' which now have turned into a '*glorious summer*' of peaceful days (I, i, ll. 1–3).
- *Personification* – an inanimate thing or an abstract idea is given human qualities in order to create a mental image
  Richard battles with his guilt: '*My conscience hath a thousand several* (= different) *tongues*' (V, iv, l. 173). In his first soliloquy, he mentions the '*grim-visaged war hath smoothed his wrinkled front*' (I, i, l. 9), which Richmond turns into '*smooth-faced peace*' (V, vii, l. 33) at the end of the play.

- *Parallelism* – the similarity of syntactical structures for dramatic effect
  Richard: '*Never came poison from so sweet a place.*' Anne: '*Never hung poison from a fouler toad*' (I, ii, ll. 147–148). The Duchess of York, saying farewell to Dorset: '*Go thou to Richmond, and good fortune guide thee!*', to Lady Anne: '*Go thou to Richard, and good angels tend thee!*' and to Queen Elizabeth: '*Go thou to sanctuary, and good thoughts possess thee!*' (IV, i, ll. 91–93).
- *Repetition* – words, phrases or clauses are repeated to emphasize their significance
  Richard's mockery of Lady Anne in I, ii, ll. 224–225: '*Was ever woman in this humour wooed? Was ever woman in this humour won?*' His frequent use of the pronoun 'myself' when struggling with his conscience shows his temporary mental derangement in V, iv, ll. 162–172. Margaret, mocking Queen Elizabeth's losses: '*Where is thy husband now? Where be thy brothers? Where are thy two sons?*' (IV, iv, ll. 92–93)
- *Simile* – a comparison of two things using 'like' or 'as'
  Buckingham compares the citizens who do not applaud his suggestion to make Richard king to stones: '*they spake not a word, but, like dumb statuès or breathing stones, stared each on other, and looked deadly pale*' (III, vii, ll. 24–26).
- *Verbal irony* – the literal meaning of what a character says does not express, or even is the opposite of, what he really means
  When the youngest prince asks Richard for his dagger, he replies '*My dagger, little cousin? With all my heart*', and 'A *greater gift than that I'll give my cousin*' (III, i, ll. 112; 116), the 'greater gift' being the death he plans for his nephew.

Imagery and evocative language

Shakespeare's plays are rich in figurative language which evokes vivid images in the minds of his listeners or readers. The ghosts' descriptions of how they died and their language of revenge conjure up the violence of past and future events (V, 4). Buckingham's remorse and acceptance of his death likewise possess great emotive power (V, 1), as do the lamentations of Queen Elizabeth's relatives who are unjustly put to death (III, 3). Other examples of language arousing the emotions of the audience are the extensive railings and colourful curses that in particular the women in the play heap on Richard. In I, 2, Lady Anne swears at him (ll. 34–186), while Margaret includes all Yorkists in her damnation (I, iii, ll. 214–244), with particular attention to Richard, though (‘*And leave out thee? Stay, dog, for thou shalt hear me*’, l. 214). In IV, 4, Richard’s mother and Queen Elizabeth both vehemently curse Richard for being who he is and for the deeds they blame on him. Emotive language can also serve as an incantation, that is, words are spoken to have a magic impact on the person they are directed at, e.g. Margaret’s damnation of Richard in I, iii, ll. 214–237. Richard’s brothers are shown as his counterparts in their use of language: Edward speaks of ‘love’, ‘peace’, ‘pardon’ and ‘brotherhood’, trying to make peace between the factions in II, 1, and Clarence, conscience-stricken, refers to ‘sin’, ‘soul’ and ‘God’ when thinking of his crimes and fate to come. In contrast, Richard expresses his irreligious attitude and vicious nature in the way he maliciously comments on others when he is alone.

Symbols

The wild boar depicted on Richard’s coat of arms represents his ferocious and relentless aggressiveness in pursuing his goals, suggesting that he is just as dangerous as this wild animal with its deadly tusks. Despite his disability, Richard is a skilled fighter who has excelled in the battles of the ‘Wars of the Roses’. After dreaming of a helmet being torn off by a boar, Stanley urges Hastings to flee with him. However, in his ill-founded trust, the unsuspecting Hastings believes ‘*the boar will use us kindly*’ (III, ii, l. 30). Richard’s enemies play the wild animal down to a mere household pig: Queen Margaret calls him ‘*elvish-marked, abortive rooting hog*’ (I, iii, l. 226) and Richmond a ‘*foul swine*’ (V, ii, l. 10). Other characters, too, compare Richard to different beasts in order to illustrate his inhuman nature (‘hedgehog’, ‘toad’, ‘dog’, ‘cur’, ‘hell-hound’, ‘spider’).

Spin doctors and their persuasive language

Richard, like Buckingham, is very adept at presenting a highly biased point of view to misinform his listeners. Using pompous language, barefaced lies and a rhetoric typical of devious politicians, Richard and

Buckingham manage to convince others for their own benefits. They use only those facts and quotations that suit their goals, deny the truth of proven facts and present unproven rumours as facts, use euphemisms, make unfounded assumptions about other people's base motives and blame them for things they did themselves. Good examples of these tactics can be found in III, 5, where they are used to justify Hastings' execution and to stage-manage a defence against attackers, or in III, 7, where Buckingham, as a 'kingmaker', prepares the Mayor and the citizens of London for Richard's appearance and tries to move them to call upon him to be their next king. Earlier, and with little success, Buckingham has already implied that the princes are bastards and claimed that Richard would be a good king. To finally win over the victims of their manipulation, the conspirators orchestrate Richard's entrance as if he happened to appear accidentally, placed between two bishops with a Bible in his hand and in apparent religious contemplation. Buckingham compares the 'pious' Richard favourably to the late King Edward, who was known to be a ladies' man, and repeats his false accusation of the princes' illegitimacy. With the help of Catesby and the Lord Mayor, Buckingham creates the impression that the crowd expressly demands Richard as their king, although all they ever say is 'Amen', when Richard finally accepts the crown. Before that, he feigns reluctance three times and consents only unwillingly, pointing out what a burden this will be for him (ll. 153–154; 164–169; 203–206; 222–235).

As a master of persuasive language, Richard can adapt his way of speaking to his respective listeners, be they children, churchmen, noblemen or townspeople, and can get them to comply with his wishes. As soon as they are out of earshot, he ridicules them as simple and gullible. Another instance of the misrepresentation of his devious motives is his courtship of Lady Anne. To begin with, he lets her take her anger out on him, endures her spitting at him and listens patiently, then modestly asks if he may excuse himself and claims he only killed her husband for the love for her. Gradually, Richard turns the conversation round, confident of the effect his words have on her. His move to hand her his sword, offering her to kill him on the spot, is well calculated, as he is rightly sure she will not have the nerve to do it. Hesitatingly, Lady Anne accepts him as her suitor and Richard crows with glee over his triumph, particularly because she will '*abase her eyes on me*' (I, ii, l. 243) after having been married to a very fine figure of a prince.

Dramatic structure and devices

In *Richard III*, there is no subplot, no romance, no humour except for Richard's own glee at his machinations. Most of the violence takes place offstage, exceptions being the stabbing of Clarence (I, 4) and Richard's final fight with Richmond in single combat (V, 7). The very first scene of the play serves not only as the exposition but also sets the plot in motion, when Richard himself informs the audience of the setting, his motivation to act and his ambition to rise in power. In the first half of the play, the audience watches Richard's manipulative tactics to murder and marry his way to the crown, while the second half dramatizes his downfall. Scene IV, 2 marks the climax or the turning-point of the play. As soon as he has become king, Richard worries about the safety of his rule and notes his weakening power. From now on, the focus is on safeguarding the throne, eliminating enemies and removing further possible contenders to the crown.

In the first act, highly emotional scenes, such as Richard's courtship of Lady Anne and the murder of Clarence, are presented in order to demonstrate the extent of Richard's wickedness. While most of the action is set in the London palace or in its surroundings, with a focus on the noble families, two so-called 'window scenes' show what is going on outside the palace, when commoners comment on the political developments and their probable effects on them (II, 3; III, 6). The last act and conclusion shows the move to the battlefields in the country near Leicester, where Richard's army meets Richmond's soldiers.

Being driven forward by talk rather than action, the plot could be seen as a didactic tale of poetic justice being served to a murderer, were it not for Richard's tremendous dramatic vitality as a ruthless powermonger, which gives him great audience appeal.

Shakespeare's handling of ***time*** contributes to the effect of fast motion in the first part of the play. Richard seems to rush events so that they work to his advantage. He courts Lady Anne as soon as her husband has died and has Clarence murdered before King Edward can pardon him. At court, he pretends that the executioners had acted upon Edward's orders and carried them out too soon. Many of Richard's victims only realize too late that he has duped them. But time is no longer in his favour when he possesses absolute power. Now, he often asks what time it is and seems to have lost control of it. Before the Battle of Bosworth, a clock strikes like an ominous sign which predicts death and the fact that the sun does not appear signifies further ill luck (V, v, ll. 6–16).

There are very few ***stage directions*** in Shakespeare's plays. Mostly, he indicates what the actors are supposed to do in their lines, e.g. when Richard addresses his mother: '*Humbly on my knee I crave your blessing.*' (II, ii, ll. 105–106)

In *Richard III*, Shakespeare has included several ***short scenes***, which have an important function in the inner logic of the play's structure. They show the repercussions Richard's deeds have on his victims (e.g. when his Woodville enemies and Buckingham are led to their deaths, remembering Margaret's curses, in III, 3 and V, 1 respectively) or illustrate what ordinary people think of the current politics (II, 3 and III, 6). Other scenes indicate the time that elapses between two events that cannot directly follow each other, such as scene III, 3 (the Woodville executions), which is placed between Hastings' warning in III, 2 and his death sentence in III, 4. Another function of these short scenes is to convey information necessary to understand the plot, such as IV, 3 (in which the young princes' death is reported) and the brief scenes showing the rival armies in their respective locations on the battlefield (V, 2; 3; 6).

Another common element in *Richard III* are predictions, either made directly by characters or expressed in the form of dreams and omens, that are fulfilled later in the play. This device, called ***foreshadowing*** (or anticipation), also occurs when characters unwittingly speak about the fate that awaits them or others or when the audience can witness actions leading to an outcome the characters themselves are unaware of. Queen Margaret calls herself a prophetess (I, iii, l. 299) and predicts grave suffering and several deaths for her enemies in I, 3, which the victims later refer to before their downfall. In IV, 4, she correctly foretells Richard's end (IV, iv, l. 74) before she leaves the country. In his dialogue with Queen Elizabeth, Richard himself names his fate unknowingly while trying to persuade her of his sincerity and the benefits of him marrying her daughter (IV, iv, ll. 397–409). Later, in V, 5, he foresees his own death at Richmond's hands, when he thinks it a bad sign that the sun has not risen or when he dismisses the note with the mocking verse ('*March on […], if not to heaven, then hand in hand to hell*', ll. 41–42). Richard also recalls a prophecy that Richmond will be his end ('*a bard of Ireland told me once I should not live long after I saw Richmond*', IV, ii, ll. 105–106).

In a dramatically highly impressive scene, eleven spirits of the characters murdered by Richard appear in succession, remind him of his misdeeds and bid him '*despair and die*' while he is sleeping before the battle against Richmond, whom they assure of their supernatural help and wish to '*live and flourish*' and be victorious (V, 4).

Elizabethans believed in the power of dreams to forecast the future, so the audience would know what to expect when characters dreamt of their deaths. In I, 4, Clarence tells his prison guard of his dream in which Richard unintentionally kills him in an accident at sea and thus unconsciously describes the mortal danger he is in. When his murderers appear, however, he does not heed this premonition and hears the killers' references to Richard in disbelief ('*You are deceived: Your brother Gloucester hates you*', I, iv, l. 223). Lord Stanley dreams of a murderous boar (Richard's emblem) and sends Lord Hastings the urgent message to flee, which he does not heed to his own fatal cost (III, 2). A tyrant like Richard evokes nightmares and also has the power to make them real.

Omens were thought to be signs of what the future held. The description of Richard already having teeth when he was born is ominous, as it makes him seem like a possible threat (II, 4, ll. 27–28). The death of King Edward, whose succession is seen with worry in the exchange of three Londoners in II, 3 ('*Woe to that land that's governed by a child*', l. 11), is equally seen with a sense of foreboding. Hastings naively manages to ignore all omens.

The dramatic device of ***atmosphere*** plays an important role in this dark tale, which contains unscrupulous politicians, sadism, cruel crimes and helpless, terrified people in a suffering country. Murders and executions are an important element of the play, but little violence is acted out on stage, although bloodier scenes would have met the taste of the time and were regularly shown in revenge tragedies. The play's mood is often solemn and dialogues ritualistic, especially when the wailing women mourn their many losses. There is also an air of myth and doom, created by the many fulfilled predictions, dreams and omens that show the power of fate. Richard's ruthless self-empowerment and his gleeful, sarcastic malevolence evoke fear and horror in the first part of the play, which is juxtaposed with his disorientation and panic caused by his loss of control over his subjects in the second part. At the end, the scenes before and during the battle convey an atmosphere of bloodshed and doom, but finally justice is served and hope returns after the usurper's defeat.

Dramatic irony is a stylistic device used by playwrights to let the audience know more than the characters on stage in order to make them feel pity or fear and to create tension. Sometimes the characters' real intentions are masked (mostly in Richard's case) or their fate is foreshadowed. Lady Anne curses Richard's future wife and thereby herself (I, ii, ll. 26–28), and Clarence says he does not want to live another night with such a bad dream as he just had before the murderers come to kill him (I, iv, ll. 2–7). Hastings boasts several times about knowing Richard and being firmly in his favour when he is clearly not (III, 2; 4). Having heard this spoken about earlier, the viewers already know that Hastings will die when Richard makes short work of him ('*Off with his head!*', III, iv, l. 76). Before the battle in which he dies, Richard remarks: '*A black day will it be to somebody.*' (V, v, l. 10) Queen Margaret has the role of a prophetess, but her warnings are ignored by all and deplored only when it is too late.

Mirroring refers to a parallel action or a similar plot in a play or to characters that try to achieve the same goal but have different traits which sometimes complement each other. This dramatic device adds complexity to a plot and shows the high dramaturgical skill of the writer who can make a point on several levels. In *Richard III*, mirroring can be seen, for example, when

- the ghosts of Richard's victims wish him defeat and victory on Richmond in the same scene (V, 4),
- or when both Richard and Richmond speak to their soldiers before the battle to encourage them, though in different ways: Richard insults the invaders as low-life creatures threatening the English nation, while Richmond claims his men have God on their side and that overthrowing Richard is a just cause (V, 5; V, 4).

In an even more intricate manner, Shakespeare mirrors matching scenes early and late in the play, in which Richard's success and failure are juxtaposed.

- Richard is cursed early by old Queen Margaret in I, 3, which he shrugs off lightly, whereas his own mother's damnation of him leaves him almost speechless, and he tries to drown out her voice with drum sounds (IV, 4).
- In his courtship of Lady Anne, he boasts about his deeds he supposedly did for love and leaves, telling her to wait for his visit. In contrast, in his talk with Queen Elizabeth about marrying her daughter in IV, 4, Richard does not appear as the same ardent lover as before, even apologizes for his deeds and leaves without any resolution of the matter.
- In two dream scenes the characters' later death is foreshadowed, first Clarence's dream that anticipates Richard's villainy in I, 4, and then Richard's own nightmare before the battle when his downfall is imminent (V, 4).

Regarding the last two examples, Shakespeare derived the later events from his sources but invented the earlier scenes for his dramatic purposes, maybe to underline the role of fate in his characters' lives or to emphasize Richard's character development.

Coping with Exam Papers

The study of *Richard III* in class will require you to write about the play either in coursework, for term papers or presentations or in final examinations. In the following part, you will find guidance on writing for different tasks.

Writing about characters

When asked to write about a ***main character***, it is advisable to follow his or her journey through the play with special attention to the moments when they change and to what exactly has influenced them to do so. Instead of compiling a list of character traits, identify individual actions that define a character and think about what they are ready to do in view of achieving their aims.

Reading only the lines these characters speak from the beginning to the end of the play and writing down the actions significant to their development will help to analyse the motivation of a protagonist. A good playwright never has his characters utter wordy dialogue for its own sake but sticks to what is important to convey about the character. Each protagonist has a "need" or "objective" he or she wants to achieve in each scene, and it is worthwhile noting what it is. Additionally, they are hindered by an obstacle or totally blocked by an antagonist and either succeed in winning against all odds or fail. This struggle creates suspense for the audience and makes watching the characters in action interesting.

Some protagonists have an overall objective that they pursue throughout the whole play, e.g. Richard, who wants to become king and secure his position, or Richmond, whose aim is to dethrone Richard.

The main characters are also placed within a social and political setting that determine their personal situations and are analysed in their respective dilemma. The Yorkists and Lancastrians get the punishment they deserve for their earlier violent actions, traitors face death sentences, and the helpless must endure the others' superiority. Either the psychology of the character can be the centre of attention (e.g. Richard's malevolent ambition) or the society they live in (e.g. women are powerless in a male-dominated society).

An analysis of ***minor characters*** is focused on what their function is in relation to a protagonist or the play's structure. Taking a closer look at Buckingham or Queen Elizabeth's contribution to the play will show their impact on the action. When asked to murder the princes, Buckingham stalls and loses his standing with Richard at once, although he has been his loyal right-hand man, which serves as a further example of Richard's cold-bloodedness. Having lost almost all of her family through Richard, Elizabeth has secretly plotted with Richmond and thus contributed to the tyrant's fall.

Comparison of characters

Another way to evaluate characters is to compare them to each other either as individuals or as characters invented for a dramatic purpose. In the section 'Language, Style and Dramatic Devices' (p. 74), a character's function as a foil or when used in mirroring is explained. Some examples are:

- The role of the women in the play / Female characters as a Greek chorus
- The different conceptions of loyalty as seen in Buckingham, Hastings and Stanley
- Conscience and remorse shown by guilty characters

The respective tasks in German final exams require comparisons drawn between characters from a literary or non-fictional text and those in the play the students have studied in class. To do so, study the information the given text offers about the characters and look for suitable points of comparison. Note down what is similar and what is different to the protagonists in the play. It is very likely that the task will not deal with minor characters. Sometimes, you are also expected to give an evaluation of the characters. In your text, explain your points of comparison and give reasons for choosing them. Begin writing your text by pointing out in which way the characters from the exam text resemble those of the play before you point out their dissimilarities. This way, your comparison will be more concise, you will avoid repetition and save time. You may point out, too, whether you think the resemblances are more important than the differences or vice versa.

Writing about the themes of a play

Each Shakespearean play deals with several themes which are exemplified on three different levels, i.e. on the personal level of the characters, on one that concerns the society or nation they live in, and on a supernatural or cosmic level. In *Richard III*, the latter is not treated as extensively as in other plays (e.g. the appearance of witches in *Macbeth* or that of his father's ghost in *Hamlet*). Here, there is only one scene with other-worldly elements, when the ghosts of Richard's victims come to curse him and wish failure on him before the decisive Battle of Bosworth against Richmond's army (V, 4).

Some of the relevant themes in *Richard III* are: appearance and reality, betrayal, justice and punishment, family conflict, good and evil, politics and ethics, chaos and order, and hierarchy in society.

When preparing your answer, point out which characters and actions are related to the theme and find short quotations to illustrate it when you are allowed to use the book. Spend some time thinking this through, because there will be more examples than first come to mind. A typical exam question could read:

> *Explain why Richard's manipulation of so many characters makes watching him fascinating in spite of his evil intentions.*

Discussing topics and writing comments

These assignments often include a quote or a statement which invites discussion on a larger scale, e.g.:

> *Discuss the extent to which modern autocratic rulers of the twentieth and twenty-first centuries are comparable to Richard III in the play of the same name.*

If you are asked to comment on an issue, you have to give your personal opinion and support or refute what the task suggests. In a discussion task, you have to look at an issue from different angles, and find pros and cons.

When you have to discuss a quote, it is required that the quote is first interpreted and explained before the actual discussion begins.

You are expected to know the contents of *Richard III* well, but you should not copy extensively from the play, nor give lengthy summaries of the contents or descriptions of the characters. To comment or discuss a topic, choose relevant details from the play to support your point. Devise a line of argument with a clear line of thought – your aim is to persuade the reader of your point of view. Quotes should only be included when they serve the argument, not just for decoration. When analysing events or characters, there should be references to the themes of the play, e.g. the importance of justice in *Richard III*.

Analysing an extract from the play or an extract from a literary or non-fictional text

Highlight what you are asked to do in the task (for the operative words, see pp. 80–81) and read the passage several times in order not to miss any important information. Many students leave out part of an assignment because they do not check the task again once they have started writing. There can be up to three different aspects that need to be dealt with in one task. Think about the context of the passage and why it has probably been chosen in the light of the study done in class during the semester so far or why an exam board might have picked it for a final examination.

Typically, there will be three sections:

1 A *comprehension question* in the form of a brief summary or outline of the passage given
2 An *analysis of the language* or stylistic devices (choice of words, connotations, syntax, imagery) and the effect this has on the reader

3a An *evaluation* in the form of a comment, a comparison or a discussion of a quote or specific aspect

or 3b A *creative writing task* referring to the play and topics raised in the extract in a prescribed text format

In a ***comprehension task*** you are expected to prove that you have understood the contents of the given extract. You are supposed to sum up in your own words either the whole text or just the required aspects. Do not include quotes from the text, examples or explanations and refrain from giving your personal opinion or adding information. The point is to sum up specific information, not to rephrase the whole text in its original length. While studying the text, divide it up into sections – you could find suitable headings for them in your draft as well. In your introductory sentence, refer briefly to the central idea of the passage and, if you deal with a non-fictional text, to the title of the text, the text type, the author's name and the source of the text.

When asked to do an ***analysis*** of the text, you have to study the underlying meaning on an abstract level and point out the means the author has used to achieve a certain effect on the reader. This can concern the structure of a text, narrative techniques (e.g. point of view, mode of presentation: showing/telling, atmosphere), stylistic devices (e.g. contrast, repetition, imagery) or the choice of words (e.g. neutral/colloquial register, tone).

Instead of listing stylistic means one after the other chronologically as they appear in the text, combine elements that belong together meaningfully when you explain their effect, e.g. how a character's fear is shown in what he does and says or what others say about him. When giving evidence from the text, quote words or short phrases with the line reference only and do not copy full sentences. Here, too, no personal comment should be added.

To learn more about writing an ***evaluation*** of a text, read what is said above in the paragraphs 'Writing about characters', 'Writing about the themes of a play' and 'Discussing topics and writing comments'.

Creative writing tasks may appear easy at first sight, but they require the same input in regard to the knowledge of the play's content and the examination of particular aspects like an evaluation task. There are several formats:

- Writing from the perspective of a character, often a bystander or a minor character of the play, e.g. a diary entry, a letter, an obituary etc.
- Devising a new scene for the play, e.g. of an offstage event or a different ending
- Writing a speech for a specific target audience to discuss a point or give a personal opinion
- Writing a letter to a newspaper editor or a person connected in some way with the topic
- Writing an article for a newspaper or magazine

Operative words

When you set about the task, find the operative words which tell you exactly what to do and highlight them with a marker. There can be several of them in one assignment and they are usually the imperative forms of a verb (= Befehlsform). Here is a list in alphabetical order:

Analyse/Examine	Describe and explain the meaning of specific aspects and their effect.
Assess/Evaluate	Reflect upon a matter carefully and give reasons for your opinion.
Comment on	Express your personal view on a matter.
Compare	Point out the similarities between things.
Contrast	Show the differences between things.
Describe	Give an account of a text using your own words.

Discuss	Examine arguments for and against a matter and draw a conclusion.
Explain	Give reasons for the causes and effects of a matter.
Illustrate	Find examples for the points you make.
Interpret	Explain the meaning of an issue and give your own view.
Outline	Give the main aspects of a text in your own words.
Point out/State	Find and explain certain points.
Summarize/Sum up	Give an account of the main points in a text.
Write	e.g. a letter, a characterization etc.

General points

- Before you start on any writing task, first collect ideas and key words in a draft (do not write full sentences here). Narrow down your material to select only what is important to the point you want to make. Then rearrange your material in a way that is meaningful to you, e.g. in a mind map, a diagram, a table or a rough outline.
- Use the simple present tense when writing about the means an author has used or about characters and situations.
- Structure your text by using paragraphs and linking words. When writing a comment or discussing a topic, refer to the task in the introduction, arrange the main body clearly (in discussions, first give the arguments you do not support, then the ones you do, with the best argument coming last) and present your personal conclusion in the last part.

- Avoid repetition and superfluous fillers like 'kind of', 'somehow', 'of course' etc.
- Put quotes into inverted commas ('…') and do not merely use them as decoration, but only to underline a point or prove an argument.
- Make life easy for your examiners by numbering pages and tasks. Make changes and additions clear with asterisks (*) or footnotes and indicated page numbers where they can find them.
- Leave sufficient time to reread your work and correct mistakes.

Written Test

Three witches prophesied Macbeth that he would one day become King of Scotland. This prompted the ambitious Macbeth to kill the reigning king and seize the throne for himself. As they also prophesied that his fellow warrior Banquo's children would be kings, he had Banquo murdered as well. When Banquo's ghost appears at a banquet, he is scared. In the scene below, he meets the witches to find reassurance about his future.

SECOND WITCH By the pricking of my thumbs,
Something wicked this way comes.
Open, locks,
Whoever knocks!

Enter MACBETH.

MACBETH How now, you secret, black, and midnight hags!
What is't you do?

ALL A deed without a name.

MACBETH I conjure you, by that which you profess,
Howe'er you come to know it, answer me:
Though you untie the winds and let them fight
Against the churches; though the yeasty waves
Confound and swallow navigation up;
Though bladed corn be lodged and trees blown down;
Though castles topple on their warders' heads;
Though palaces and pyramids do slope
Their heads to their foundations; though the treasure
Of nature's germens tumble all together,
Even till destruction sicken; answer me
To what I ask you.

FIRST WITCH Speak.

SECOND WITCH Demand.

THIRD WITCH We'll answer.

FIRST WITCH Say, if thou'dst rather hear it from our mouths,
Or from our masters?

MACBETH Call 'em; let me see 'em.

FIRST WITCH Pour in sow's blood, that hath eaten
Her nine farrow; grease that's sweaten
From the murderer's gibbet throw
Into the flame.

ALL Come, high or low;
Thyself and office deftly show!

Thunder. Enter FIRST APPARITION, an armed Head.

MACBETH Tell me, thou unknown power, --

FIRST WITCH He knows thy thought:
Hear his speech, but say thou nought.

FIRST APPARITION Macbeth! Macbeth! Macbeth! Beware Macduff;
Beware the Thane of Fife. Dismiss me. Enough.
Descends

MACBETH Whate'er thou art, for thy good caution, thanks;
Thou hast harped my fear aright: but one word more, --

FIRST WITCH He will not be commanded: here's another,
More potent than the first.

Thunder. Enter SECOND APPARITION, a bloody Child.

SECOND APPARITION Macbeth! Macbeth! Macbeth!

MACBETH Had I three ears, I'd hear thee.

SECOND APPARITION Be bloody, bold, and resolute; laugh to
scorn
The power of man, for none of woman born
Shall harm Macbeth. *Descends*

MACBETH Then live, Macduff: what need I fear of thee?
But yet I'll make assurance double sure,
And take a bond of fate: thou shalt not live;
That I may tell pale-hearted fear it lies,
And sleep in spite of thunder.

Thunder. Enter THIRD APPARITION: a Child crowned, with a tree in his hand.

What is this
That rises like the issue of a king,
And wears upon his baby-brow the round
And top of sovereignty?

ALL Listen, but speak not to't.

THIRD APPARITION Be lion-mettled, proud; and take no care
Who chafes, who frets, or where conspirers are:
Macbeth shall never vanquished be until
Great Birnam wood to high Dunsinane hill
Shall come against him. *Descends*

MACBETH That will never be
Who can impress the forest, bid the tree
Unfix his earth-bound root? Sweet bodements! Good!
Rebellion's head, rise never till the wood
Of Birnam rise, and our high-placed Macbeth
Shall live the lease of nature, pay his breath
To time and mortal custom. Yet my heart
Throbs to know one thing: tell me, if your art

Can tell so much: shall Banquo's issue ever
Reign in this kingdom?

ALL Seek to know no more.

MACBETH I will be satisfied: deny me this,
And an eternal curse fall on you! Let me know.
Why sinks that cauldron? And what noise is this?

FIRST WITCH Show!

SECOND WITCH Show!

THIRD WITCH Show!

ALL Show his eyes, and grieve his heart;
Come like shadows, so depart!

A show of eight KINGS, the last with a glass in his hand; the GHOST OF BANQUO following.

MACBETH Thou art too like the spirit of Banquo: down!
Thy crown does sear mine eye-balls. And thy hair,
Thou other gold-bound brow, is like the first.
A third is like the former. Filthy hags!
Why do you show me this? A fourth! Start, eyes!
What, will the line stretch out to th' crack of doom?
Another yet! A seventh! I'll see no more:
And yet the eighth appears, who bears a glass
Which shows me many more; and some I see
That two-fold balls and treble sceptres carry:
Horrible sight! Now, I see, 'tis true;
For the blood-boltered Banquo smiles upon me,
And points at them for his. *APPARITIONS vanish*
What, is this so?

FIRST WITCH Ay, sir, all this is so: but why
Stands Macbeth thus amazedly?
Come, sisters, cheer we up his sprites,
And show the best of our delights:
I'll charm the air to give a sound,
While you perform your antic round:
That this great king may kindly say,
Our duties did his welcome pay.

Music. The WITCHES dance, and then vanish.

MACBETH Where are they? Gone? Let this pernicious hour
Stand aye accursèd in the calendar! Come in, without
there!

Enter LENNOX.

LENNOX What's your grace's will?

MACBETH Saw you the weird sisters?

LENNOX No, my lord.

MACBETH Came they not by you?

LENNOX No, indeed, my lord.

MACBETH Infected be the air whereon they ride;
And damned all those that trust them! I did hear
The galloping of horse: who was't came by?

LENNOX 'Tis two or three, my lord, that bring you word
Macduff is fled to England.

MACBETH Fled to England!

LENNOX Ay, my good lord.

MACBETH Time, thou anticipat'st my dread exploits:
The flighty purpose never is o'ertook
Unless the deed go with it; from this moment
The very firstlings of my heart shall be
The firstlings of my hand. And even now,
To crown my thoughts with acts, be it thought and done:
The castle of Macduff I will surprise;
Seize upon Fife; give to the edge o' the sword
His wife, his babes, and all unfortunate souls
That trace him in his line. No boasting like a fool;
This deed I'll do before this purpose cool.
But no more sights! Where are these gentlemen?
Come, bring me where they are.

Exeunt

Annotations

1 pricking: slight tingling pain **6** hag: ugly and unpleasant old woman **9** conjure: demand; profess: claim **11** though: even if **12** yeasty: having a mass of small bubbles on top **13** confound: smash up; navigation: ships at sea **14** bladed corn be lodged: ripening corn is blown down **15** warder: keeper, guard **16** slope: bend (i.e. collapse) **17–18** though the treasure … together: if the seeds of life are thrown into chaos **19** sicken: become weary **24** if thoud'st: if you would **27** sow: female pig **28** farrow: piglets; sweaten: sweated **29** gibbet: post from which murderers were hung **32** thyself and office: you and your role; deftly: skilfully **36** nought: nothing **37** beware: be warned of **38** Macduff: a nobleman of Scotland **39** Thane: old Scottish title of honour (Earl); Fife: area which Macduff rules **41** caution: care **42** harped my fear aright: guessed my worries correctly **45** potent: powerful **49** resolute: determined; laugh to scorn: don't take seriously **55** take a bond of fate: swear an oath / make sure fate keeps its promise **56** that I may: so that I will be able to; pale-hearted: cowardly **61** issue: child, offspring **62–63** the round and top of sovereignty: the crown **65** lion-mettled: brave as a lion **66** chafe: argue; fret: worry (about Macbeth's rule); conspirer: conspirator, a person involved in a secret plan **67** vanquished: defeated **68** high Dunsinane hill: the location of Macbeth's castle **71** impress: give an order to, force to join an army **72** bodement: prophecy **75–76** live the lease of nature … custom: die a natural death, live as long as nature lets you **77** throb: beat strongly; art: skills **83** cauldron: large deep pot **89** so: in the same way **90** glass: mirror **93** sear: burn **94** gold-bound brow: crowned head **96** start: jump out of your eye-sockets **97** th'crack of doom: the thunder supposed to sound on Doomsday, the Day of Judgement **101** two-fold balls … sceptres: symbols of a ruler **103** blood-boltered: smothered in blood **104** for his: as his descendants **108** sprite: spirit **111** antic round: crazy, unnatural dance **113** our duties did his welcome pay: we treated him with respect and did as he asked **115** pernicious: dangerous, harmful **116** aye accursèd: forever cursed; come in, without there: calling another thane who was waiting nearby **118** Lennox: nobleman of Scotland **120** weird sister: witch **131** anticipat'st my dread exploits: have guessed my fearsome deeds **132–133** the flighty purpose … with it: planning an action without doing it at once is not good **134–135** the very firstlings … of my hand: from now on I will act on my first impulse **138** surprise: attack **139** give to … sword: kill **141** trace him in his line: are his descendants **142** before this purpose cool: immediately **143** sight: vision

Tasks

CONTENT

1. Outline the situation and the conversation in this excerpt.

LANGUAGE

2 a. Analyse Macbeth's language (sentence structure, verse, stylistic devices, imagery etc.) to show how Shakespeare creates character and describes the range of feelings Macbeth goes through.

2 b. Examine the language of the witches, ghosts and apparitions (verse, stylistic devices, imagery etc.) and point out how it contributes to the atmosphere in the scene and its dramatic effect.

DISCUSSION

3. In the night before the Battle of Bosworth, King Richard has an encounter with ghosts. Compare and contrast the actions of the supernatural beings and witches in both scenes as well as Macbeth's and Richard's experiences and reactions to them.

Expected answers

1. Macbeth challenges the witches to answer his questions, even if it has negative consequences for him. They agree and offer him to hear their prophecies directly from their masters, which he accepts. They conjure up a succession of apparitions, which all appear with thunder. Macbeth wants to question them but is told not to speak as they can hear his thoughts. The first apparition, an armed head, warns him of Macduff, the Thane of Fife. When the second apparition, a bloody child, has foretold him that no naturally born man can endanger him, Macbeth is content but, to feel completely safe, resolves to kill Macduff anyway. A crowned child holding a tree predicts that Macbeth will only be defeated when Birnam Wood approaches his castle. Feeling relieved because a wood cannot move, Macbeth believes himself safe until he dies a natural death. The witches initially refuse to answer more questions, but Macbeth threatens to curse them and wants to

know whether Banquo's children will ever be kings. They then show him a procession of eight kings wearing crowns and Banquo's ghost which smiles at him. One of the kings is holding a mirror whose reflection shows even more of Banquo's descendants. Mocking Macbeth's dismay, the witches dance and disappear while Macbeth expresses his anger about their prophecies. When Lennox informs him that Macduff has fled, Macbeth decides to have all of Macduff's family killed and always to act on his first impulse at once in future.

2 a. When Macbeth arrives, his tone is bold and commanding, even insulting, because of his desire to hear more prophecies ('*How now, you secret, black, and midnight hags!*', l. 6; 'I *conjure you … answer me to what I ask you*', ll. 9, 19–20; '*Call 'em, let me see 'em*', l. 26). Listing with vivid mental images what powers the witches can set free when they '*untie the winds*' (l.11), he characterizes himself as a courageous man daring to meet them, but also paying respect to their force of evil. Their turbulent winds are so powerful that they can ruin crops, bend and topple buildings, sink ships at sea and cause utter destruction for all life-giving elements (ll. 11–19). Although he is repeatedly told to listen and not to speak to the apparitions (ll. 35–36, 64), Macbeth can still not refrain from addressing them and treating them like equals ('*Tell me, thou unknown power*', l. 34; '*Whate'er thou art … but one word more*', ll. 41–43; '*Had I three ears, I'd hear thee*', l. 48), which shows his impatience or curiosity. He comments on the predictions eagerly and interprets them positively to fight his fear ('*Then live, Macduff … thunder*', ll. 53–57; '*That will never be … mortal custom*', ll. 70–76). He marvels at the looks of the apparitions (ll. 60–64), though he is not intimidated. After having been warned of Macduff, he is relieved when he hears that '*none of woman born*' (l. 51) will pose a threat to him. Displaying utter ruthlessness, Macbeth decides to kill Macduff anyway, just to be on the safe side (ll. 53–57). Interpreting the second apparition, Macbeth gladly concludes that as a wood cannot change its position, he need not worry about any threat. Apparently, he has no suspicion that the predictions might have a double meaning or should not be taken at face value. Unafraid of their magic powers, he commands the witches again and threatens to curse them (ll. 81–82) when they refuse further information. But when the parade of crowned ghosts is conjured up,

the change in Macbeth's language shows his shock and awe. His measured verse becomes more fragmented, the rhythm is abrupt, and his speech contains exclamations and questions. He refers to the kings one by one using ordinal numbers and mentions their crowns, orbs and sceptres and the reflection of even more of Banquo's descendants in a mirror (ll. 92–102). His own amazement is shown with words that describe sight and his reaction to what is shown (e.g. '*Thy crown does sear mine eye-balls*', l. 93; '*Start, eyes!*', l. 96; '*Horrible sight!*', l. 102). He angrily comments on the witches' mocking farewell: '*Let this pernicious hour stand aye accursèd in the calendar!*' (ll. 115–116). But in his last speech, Macbeth's tone and choice of words suggest that he is calmer and feels totally confident and in control again. He curses the '*weird sisters*' (l. 120) and refuses to trust their prophecies ('*Infected be the air whereon they ride; and damned all of them that trust them!*', ll. 124–125). He speaks with Lennox in a matter-of-fact tone and is no longer influenced by the emotions he felt earlier. When he hears of Macduff's flight, Macbeth determines to follow his instinct more quickly from now on to prevent his plans from failing. His longer and measured sentences suggest a calmer state of mind. His cold-blooded murderous intention to eliminate Macduff's whole family is expressed even more forcefully by the use of rhyme: '*No boasting like a fool; this deed I'll do before this purpose cool.*' (ll. 141–142)

2 b. The witches often speak in a group as if reciting a ritual and use rhyme and tetrameter (eight syllables to a line) when they cast spells ('*Pour in sow's blood … deftly show!*', ll. 27–32; '*Show his eyes and grieve his heart; come like shadows, so depart!*', ll. 88–89) or address and ridicule Macbeth (ll. 1–4, 106–113). Thus, their words have the effect of an incantation. It is made clear before he enters that they feel no sympathy for him ('*Something wicked this way comes*', l. 2). For effect and to create an air of mystery and magic, they speak short words in quick succession: '*Speak. Demand. We'll answer*' (ll. 21–23) and say '*Show*' three times when they evoke the spirits (ll. 84–86). In the first part of the dialogue, they only "shush" Macbeth and do not threaten him with their powers for instance. But after they have presented Banquo's dynasty, they mock Macbeth face to face, using irony ('*Ay, sir, all this is so … welcome pay*', ll. 106–113) and pretending they want to cheer him up

with a dance. In contrast, the apparitions use blank verse and pentameter (ten syllables to a line) in their prophecies. To make their utterances impressive, they call Macbeth's name three times in exclamations (ll. 37, 45) and use warning words like '*Beware*' (l. 37). Their outward appearances symbolize their spoken messages, illustrating fighting (armed head), birth (bloody child) and a threatening forest (crowned child with a tree). They often use imperatives (ll. 37–38, 49–50, 64–65) and the future tense in accordance with the prophetic nature of their words ('*none shall … harm*', l. 51–52; '*shall never vanquished be*', l. 67). The ghosts, on the other hand, remain silent and thus form a striking contrast to the witches and apparitions. Together with Macbeth's verbal expressions, this extremely diverse use of dialogue makes this an impressive theatrical experience on the level of language alone. Artfully costumed witches that predict the future while magically evoking apparitions and ghosts lend a mood of foreboding, horror and doom to any theatrical scene, especially when they throw disgusting items into a boiling cauldron. The apparitions and ghosts wear equally fanciful costumes and add to the atmosphere of superstition and fear. Sending nine non-speaking actors in identical clothes in a line across the stage creates a powerful effect in itself. Macbeth appears as a kind of commentator on the show that is meant to ridicule him and allows Banquo an act of retaliation.

3. Both Richard and Macbeth experience supernatural phenomena in remote areas far away from their castles: Macbeth in Scotland in a place where witches cast their spells and Richard in Bosworth Field near Leicester, where a decisive battle will be fought the next day. In both cases, the atmosphere is tense, frightening and foreboding, and the men find themselves in a moment of crisis, one worrying about the safety of his crown and the other defending his throne. A large group of ghosts appears in both situations, though they come unbidden in Richard's case and curse him severely while he is sleeping, whereas Macbeth has gone to see the witches on purpose. While ghostly kings show Macbeth that he will not have royal heirs, Richard's spirits are those of his own victims whose deaths he ordered or whom he murdered himself. The messages the ghosts convey are devastating for both kings, although Richard's ghosts take the trouble to reproach him

with his crimes individually, wish him defeat in the upcoming battle and promise his Lancastrian enemy Richmond victory and supernatural support, even from the Yorkist faction among them. Macbeth also sees three apparitions which rise and descend after the witches' charm, warning the king and predicting his future with unusual images ('*none of woman born*', '*moving forest*'). He interprets all predictions in his favour, not suspecting any ambiguity or threat. However, when he asks if Banquo's children will reign Scotland in future, they enter in a silent procession wearing royal insignia, and mocking hints are made that Banquo's lineage is even longer than that. Macbeth is horrified, just like Richard who wakes up shaken by his nightmare. Unknowingly, Richard also foresees the moment before his death after losing his horse in combat. This is the only scene in the play that shows Richard's insecurity and admission of guilt. Unlike Richard, Macbeth reveals no deep-felt crisis of confidence, but is first shocked and then angered by the ghostly kings' parade and the witches' dance. Richard is so shaken by the spirits' curses that he even tells Ratcliffe how much this vision has upset him, though he has never been conscience-stricken by his bloody deeds before. In a moment of self-realization, Richard thinks nobody will mourn him. After some soul-searching, he concludes that he will continue being a villain and fight to the bitter end, just like Macbeth, who will disregard the prophecies made and wipe out Macduff's family only because of his desertion. In the end, both men, although strong, are victims of evil powers beyond their control.